ing inspire others to see th... ...lissa
and serve others; make a d... ...vhile
rlds—earning and living w... ...ign.
nd living up to the challeng... ...given potential. It's
ng hired to help someone else realize theirs. It's also time
iends and family." — Michelle Daugherty • "It is about
lse's rules and regulations for my life. It is about the rare
nore, and give more than I ever thought possible. Making
the ability to see possibility in situations instead of limi-
ly. Lastly, I love having the privilege of leaving a legacy.
ng a life, not just a living" is about doing what I love and

TO MAKE A LIFE?

king money is great, as it provides options. Making a life
we can never create more time, so having the freedom to
e ultimate blessing is when we can gift our time and re-
ng a life!" — Michele Pitto • "Creating a home-centered
pursue my God given passion of impacting the lives of
very single day. Whether it is serving my family, friends,
st that they can be, I continue to grow daily. Sometimes
erseverance. I have found that my personal growth = life
nd of my life God will say, 'Well done my good & faith-
nendously blessed by God, so that I might bless others.'
other toward love and good deeds.'" — Sharron Rankin

MAKE A
LIFE
not just a living

Curt Beavers

Among the people who shared their stories for this book are the following leaders in our business. I am grateful for their help. If you would like to know more or connect with them, please contact them.

Kerry Daigle	keeppunching1@gmail.com
Wendy Campbell	wendycnmd@gmail.com
Mick Daly	mick@dalys.com
Jenny Daly	jp@dalys.com
Kathrine Lee	Kathrine@PureHopeFoundation.com
Michelle Barnett	michebarnett@gmail.com

Text copyright © 2016 by Curt Beavers
Written in collaboration with Dick Parker

Published by Looking Glass Books, Inc.
Decatur, Georgia

Printed in the United States
ISBN 978-1-929619-64-1

For my wife and best friend, Lori. Together we are making a wonderful life.

For our children—Trey and his wife, Katie; Hope; and Zach—who are seeking their purpose, following their passion, and making their lives.

For my mom, who poured everything she had into me.

For my pastor, Buddy Hoffman, and Grace Fellowship Church, a body of believers that surrounds Lori and me with love as we do life together every day.

For Jay Martin and the Juice Plus Company for providing the platform from which we are making a life.

And for my Heavenly Father, who revealed Himself through kairos moments and guided me in the Way to make a life, not just a living.

Introduction

Some people think of life as a journey.

Life, I believe, is a mission. Each of us has been given particular skills, assets, opportunities, and relationships to fulfill that mission. We feel a unique passion for certain people or to respond to particular opportunities.

When we live in the intersection of our skills, our passion and purpose, and the world's need, then we are making a life, not just a living.

Make a Life, Not Just a Living offers more inspiration than instruction. In my life I've been inspired by some of the people closest to me, beginning with my mother, to seek God's purpose for my life. When I was young, she fed me Proverbs and cereal for breakfast every morning, giving me the wisdom of the words themselves while teaching me the importance of seeking that wisdom every morning.

Later, when my father was no longer a regular

part of my life, godly men stepped up to mentor and guide me. And when my wife, Lori, and I started our Juice Plus Virtual Franchise, I was inspired by great people in our business who used the opportunities they created in the company to pursue their passion.

It started with an incredible opportunity to share clean water through an amazing filtration product that added air filtration and now Juice Plus, the largest whole food nutrition product in the world. Their mission of "inspiring healthy living around the world" has fulfilled company president Jay Martin's dream to "build a stable and lasting company that helps as many people as possible realize their dreams." It has helped many "make a life, not just a living."

Pursue your passion, and God will make your mission clear to you.

Then make a life, not just a living.

Contents

ONE
Start with "Why"

I WAS THIRTEEN years old when my parents' marriage fell apart and my father was forced into bankruptcy.

Dad had taken his furniture business public a few years earlier and continued to grow it with financial leverage. We lived in a big house on the north side of Atlanta near the Chattahoochee River and took month-long vacations on Sea Island. Then Dad agreed with a large developer to furnish an apartment complex. Dad borrowed money and bought the furniture, then the economy tanked and the deal fell through. Beavers Furniture Company, the company my grandfather had started decades earlier, was gone. In a matter of months, everything was swept away.

On top of financial troubles, my parents were not holding their marriage together, though I would not understand that until I was older. Difficult finances have a way of magnifying other problems. Dad took a job that required him to travel every week. He was doing all he could to refill the bank account, but the hole was too deep.

Then the bank foreclosed on our house, and Mom withdrew my brother and me from the prestigious private school we attended in northwest Atlanta.

With no income or prospects, Mom felt totally alone and panicked over how she would ever put food on the table and shoes on my brother's and my feet. She didn't have any place to take us but my grandparents' fishing cabin. So we moved to Gainesville, Georgia, for a season. Through the church we joined, we met a home builder who had a house that hadn't sold, and he let us live there rent free. Technically, Mom and Dad were still married, but he took a job that kept him on the road all the time, and he was not around very much. And then he and Mom divorced.

Mom worked a job in a paint store for a short time, then she used her creative skills in interior decorating. She wasn't suited for either job, but she threw all her passion into her work because of her love for my brother and me. Still, we were barely making it, even with a free house.

I didn't understand at the time how difficult it must have been for her to leave us to go to work every day. I was in middle school, so it wasn't like she was leaving toddlers at home, and yet there would be days when she had to go out early and come home late, and as a parent now I know that was hard.

✝ ✝ ✝

Love your spouse in front of your kids.

Let your kids know the importance of God in

your life. Pursue God in front of them.

Model a good work ethic.

✝ ✝ ✝

Adding to her worry, when I was twelve Mom feared I might lose a leg. A strange lump appeared on my knee, and when our doctor looked at it, he immediately sent me to a surgeon. They took X-rays and did some other tests, then scheduled me for surgery at once. Mom was terrified, though she didn't let me know. That was about the same time Edward Kennedy Jr., who was my age, had his right leg amputated because of bone cancer. The lump on my knee turned out to be benign, but the experience with the surgeon and the hospital left a deep impression on both Mom and me. She wanted to protect me, and I wanted to do what my doctors were doing—fix problems. I admired their professionalism and was attracted by the respect they experienced in the hospital.

While Mom worked to earn money to take care of us, my grandmother became like a mother for my brother and me, cooking for us or taking me to tennis practice or other activities. She was of the generation where they had a garden and they cooked. I always loved going to Grandma's because I got a good home-cooked meal, and she always had fresh-prepared food in the kitchen, whether it was green beans and okra, chocolate cake, macaroni and cheese, or country fried steak. The next morning she'd get up and make home-made biscuits for breakfast.

My grandparents were the definition of a "working-class" family. My grandfather had worked the night shift at the General Motors assembly plant following the Depression, and didn't retire from GM until fifty years later. He had attended high school, but I don't know if he graduated.

He could build anything, and he and my grandmother grew a lot of their food in the garden. My grandmother worked as a nurse, and when they saved enough money, they bought the cabin we later stayed in up on Lake Lanier north of Atlanta. My grandfather remodeled it himself and later retired there. He taught me about plumbing, framing, and electrical work by letting me work alongside him. He modeled hard work for me. He wasn't a pro, but he figured things out.

Even though my grandparents' cabin was right on the lake, they didn't live a typical lake life. They had an old boat that never worked. My grandfather could fix anything on a car and anything in the house, but for some reason he never got around to fixing the boat. So we fished off the dock for catfish, usually in the evening. And we never stayed out there too late. My grandparents went to bed early and woke up early—before the sun. Technically my grandfather was retired, but he never stopped working on stuff.

AN AT-RISK KID

On paper I was a classic at-risk teenage boy. I hardly ever saw my father. My mother worked full time. Our world has changed so much from the days when multiple generations of families lived in the same town or worked in the family business together—having a father as a living model every day. I did not. And we were living in a new community where I didn't know a soul.

Our church became the centerpiece of my life. Several men there saw a kid without a dad at home, who needed a strong, positive adult role model, and they reached out to me. Our minister Tom Grady, youth pastor Steve Brown, and Sunday school teacher Reuben Black, as well as a businessman, Art Kunzer, who hired me for my first job, were all at church on Sundays supporting, encouraging, and influencing me. Because my mom worked, I went on every mission trip and every youth camp and retreat the church offered. She knew I was in a safe place.

I'm so grateful that my Heavenly Father filled the gaps when I was growing up without seeing my earthly father day to day. God is the hope to the fatherless. Even as a teenager I began to realize God had a plan for my life—a plan for an abundant life, even though I didn't know what that would look like geographically or professionally. He gave me hope.

To this day, I love my church. My world centers around that community. The most difficult times in my life have been when we changed churches and I didn't have a church home for a time. The importance of the church family in my life started in high school.

If I wasn't at home, church, or school, I was on the tennis court, sometimes for four hours a day. Coach Walters taught English at my high school and really cared about people and kids. Coach Walters was a tough teacher; he required his students to work hard, so a lot of kids didn't like him. But after school he would play tennis with me. He had lost an eye years earlier, and he had an unorthodox swing. He never tried to coach me, but he was a great tennis player. I learned a lot just being on the court with him. I knew he cared about me, and that mattered.

Teenagers can learn so much confidence when they work summer jobs, and Ryland Scott made sure I would always feel confident around technology. Mr. Scott (he and his wife were in a Bible study with Mom) gave me a summer job with his computer company when I was a high school senior. I had never taken a computer class, but he immersed me in the business, showing me how to make repairs to customers' machines. I've never been intimidated by computers since then.

These men and others poured into me in ways that, looking back, remind me of Paul, Timothy, and Barnabas in the early Christian church. Paul and Barnabas were running mates, shoulder to shoulder. Then Paul had young Timothy, whom he mentored, and Timothy had Paul, the wise sage, to teach, support, and encourage him.

✝ ✝ ✝

God works by nudging our hearts, and He brings people together for a reason. He often gives us one of these roles—mentor/encourager, running mate, or learner—in our relationships with the people He has brought into our lives.

✝ ✝ ✝

Mom had been working for two years in retail and decorating when her friend Grace Kinser told her about a direct-sales cosmetics company and encouraged her to join. Mom liked the product and she liked the idea of building a team to sell with her. For the first time, she was on a mission.

Mission is an important word here. People will follow you if they think you're going somewhere. If they think you're going nowhere, they don't want to go there with you. They want a target. A destination. The mission you commit yourself to tells them where you're going. Mom began selling cosmetics and invited some of her friends to join her. They did, and then they invited their friends. Almost all of the women who joined her in the beginning had been in her Bible study or church. They prayed before every meeting. For the first time Mom's passion for taking care of her sons was joined with a mission as she invited her friends to join her.

HUNGRY FOR SOMETHING MORE

Everybody who succeeds in our business hungers to do more with their life. They're hungry way beyond punching a clock and getting paid. I remember the women Mom connected with at the company, and they remind me of our team at Juice Plus. The common thread among them is a hunger that wasn't being satisfied where they formerly worked. They were making a living. They were out there in a rut, doing their thing. Maybe they didn't want to fly every week, didn't want to travel so much, didn't want to be gone from home, didn't want to sit in rush hour traffic every day. Maybe they wanted to send their kids to a better school, or they wanted something as simple as a new car or as big as a new life.

Then they overcame the belief that they didn't

have enough money to start a business. Nobody has less money than my mother did when she started her cosmetics business. She didn't have anything. But she learned that she had something more valuable for starting a business than financial capital. She had relational capital—friends who believed in her and trusted her and had a "why" of their own. Over time people close to my mom saw this business take her from scarcity to abundance. They knew other people were in a financial hole, and the business became a ladder they could lower into that hole for other people to climb out.

WHEN THE WHY IS STRONG ENOUGH

During that time Mom came across a statement from Holocaust survivor Viktor Frankl, who wrote in his book *Man's Search for Meaning* that when the why is strong enough, the how-to will come.

Mom embraced that statement because it described her so well. When Dad left and she hit rock bottom and cried out to God for help, her "why" was to take care of her family. She would have endured anything for us. But she didn't have to. Her natural gifts for making friends and building a community created an opportunity that suited her perfectly.

Each of us has a desire for something bigger than

ourselves—family, church, community, country, the world. That desire is the beginning of making a life. It's our "why."

RELATIONAL CAPITAL

The day Mom started her new business, I was her assistant. I was fifteen by then, and I ran her warehouse and kept up with inventory. When I turned sixteen, I drove a delivery truck from Atlanta to Athens, taking products to her sales team. When they had meetings, I hauled boxes and gallons of aloe vera down the steps and to the cars. I knew all these women, took their checks, reconciled the cash register, everything.

My mother and her friends were the first to show me the power of relational capital for pursuing a mission or building a business. They wouldn't have used that term when they were starting out nearly forty years ago (and neither did I), but it was obvious that their friendships, loyalty, influence, respect, and trust in each other were key to their success. Many of the women that Mom connected with to sell cosmetics were longtime friends, neighbors, and Bible study companions.

In a business like ours, you come alongside each relationship and let them know you care, and then as that connection grows stronger, you can do more together. Mom had already built a relationship of trust with the people starting out with her. As the business grew, she established new relationships, earned their trust, and broadened her relational capital.

✢ ✢ ✢

Nobody cares how much you know until

they know how much you care.

✢ ✢ ✢

Mom learned that each of these women had a reason—a "why"—for selling cosmetics that was greater than simply making money. Their reasons for joining Mom in the business were complex. They wanted to help Mom financially, but that alone wasn't enough motivation. They could have found easier ways to help her. To use the old proverb, they wanted to teach her to fish, not just give her a fish.

They liked the product (nobody is going to sell with integrity if they don't believe in the product or the service they're providing), but there must have been hundreds of other products they liked that they didn't sell.

A few of them, like Mom, needed money, while others were more than comfortable with their current income. One friend was helping support her family while her husband was in seminary. Another wanted to help small churches across north Georgia buy stained-glass windows. Mom had her own passion for our family—that we not fall into poverty.

As the women understood each others' motivations, then they celebrated all of the successes—not just their own. Mom poured everything she could into those women, and they poured back into her. That is the impact of relational capital.

I learned from them that relationships are much more important than any bank balance, any savings account, or any super-duper time-management program. You can build any business anywhere in the world if you have the relational capital to do it.

People buy a product because you ask them, not just because the product is sitting there. You build enough trust for them to spend a certain amount on a product you recommend. If they use the product and like it, their trust in you grows. Then their positive experience, shared with others, becomes the impetus for others to benefit.

A MENTOR STEPS UP

When I began helping Mom with her business, I needed a mentor to show me how to do life. I had learned a lot working in a store alongside the owner, but helping my mother start a new business was much more intimidating. I needed guidance. Our friend Gary O'Malley stepped up. Gary was a corporate trainer who created and facilitated programs for Fortune 500 companies across the country. He was a master at time management, and his passion was helping people discover their unique gifts and God's purpose for their lives.

Gary was another one of those men with an intuition for young people who need a positive role model in their lives. The first thing he talked to me about was the importance of quiet time every morning. Gary began every day in quiet time with an open Bible, and he encouraged me to do the same—to let God fill my tank so that I could pour out God that day instead of pouring out of myself. That concept wasn't easy to understand as a teenager.

Then he shared the time-management principles he was teaching to professionals at Fortune 500 companies. I was probably the only student in Johnson High School who carried a Franklin Planner. I managed my calendar and my contacts in the back of the book. I didn't realize it at the time, but Gary was teaching me to make a life by putting my focus on God first thing every morning, discovering God's purpose for my life, and managing my time and responsibilities so they didn't overwhelm me.

About the same time I heard a pastor make an analogy using Lee Iacocca, the most widely respected American businessman at the time. Iacocca was credited with saving Chrysler Corporation by reorganizing the company and introducing the minivan in the United States.

These were my impressionable years, so I perked up when a pastor asked in a sermon, "What if Lee Iacocca offered to do a call with you every morning so he could teach you the ways of the car industry?"

Who wouldn't jump at the chance? I thought back on the mentors who had guided me and wondered what it would be like to have a giant of American industry take me under his wing.

Then the pastor continued, "You know what? You have a much better opportunity than that, because God says, 'If you'll be still and quiet, I'll meet you early each morning, and I will teach you the ways of this kingdom I've created.'"

Instantly that statement became an anchor that I could count on. I never forgot the illustration. I'm not living in my world or Lee Iacacco's world. I'm living in God's world, and who better to teach me how to live in the world but the One who created it. So I determined to spend more time with Him and get on His plan, not mine.

Then Henry Blackaby's *Experiencing God* workbook reinforced my understanding that this is God's world. Blackaby wrote that you should not ask God to join you in the world you are creating, but instead, figure out what God is doing and join Him there. I can make no plan as big and as exciting as the plans God has created.

Where can I learn about that plan?

— In my quiet time.

— From the Bible.

— In prayer.

— Through the influence of godly people.

And that was hard for me, because I don't always wait and listen patiently. Gary had started me on a morning discipline, and I was ready for God to use that time to show me His plan for my life. Yet I wanted to do more than just start this process. I wanted God to jump up with a neon sign and say, "Here's the life I want you to make. Here's the map. Here's the sign. Now go do this!"

Instead, God said, "Wait, and then I will show you

what is next. Just one step."

Then He told me to break down the boundaries I had created. Stop saying, "God, I'll go with You as long as You don't ask me to ..."

God says, "I don't do boundaries, because I have no boundaries. My plans for you are beyond every boundary you can imagine. Trust Me. Follow Me."

In that moment God shared with me almost audibly, "If you take care of My business, I'll take care of your business."

God took care of Mom's business (and later Lori's and mine) in ways we never imagined. That phone call from Grace Kinser changed the trajectory of our family's life forever. The whole time Mom was working in the cosmetics business, I was in the middle of it—less after I went to college, but when I came home for summer and holidays, I worked with her. I really learned a respect for the industry—the industry we're in today. I saw my mom go from having nothing to achieving professional success, as well as creating a platform to share her mission.

A GOOD LIFE OR A GREAT LIFE?

Soon after I graduated from high school, the cosmetics company asked Mom to move to Atlanta to become a regional vice president. They bought a home for her to live in and a car for her to drive. I enrolled at Emory University in pre-med, following the path I had started on when I had knee surgery five years earlier. I planned to finish college and medical school and become an orthopedic surgeon.

Then during my sophomore year at Emory, my grandfather went to the hospital with a tumor behind his ear, and I began to understand the importance of "why." His growth was not cancer, but while he was in the hospital he contracted spinal meningitis, which sent him to the intensive care unit for weeks.

Someone from our family was at the hospital constantly throughout his time there, and I spent many, many hours in the ICU visiting my grandfather, talking with his nurses and his surgeon. If I was at the hospital early in the morning, I met the doctor making her early-morning rounds. If I was there in the evening, I would see the surgeon making rounds again, sometimes still in her scrubs after a day of surgery. She said she usually got home around eight o'clock at night. But she said she had a great life—a beautiful house, a cool car, two country club memberships, all the trappings of financial success.

Every day I watched her and listened to her talk about the demands of her work, and I became more convinced that if I stayed in school another ten years to become a surgeon, I would be a gerbil on a spinning wheel in a cage, making tons of money, but having no way to express a great life. The house, the cars, the country club were all fine, but she appeared to have left no time to enjoy those things. I couldn't imagine the stress she was living under every day.

God had put that surgeon in front of me and said, "This is what you're planning to do. Is this the life you want?"

By the time my grandfather went home from the hospital, I had made up my mind. I transferred to Georgia Tech and got a business degree. I didn't know what I would do, but medicine looked like a grind that I wanted no part of.

Please understand, those men and women who are called to the medical profession are a godsend, and we must be grateful for them. Any profession can have a similar impact on people who don't create and respect boundaries. At the other end of the financial spectrum, construction workers sometimes work eighty-four hours a week—seven straight twelve-hour days. They earn forty-four hours of overtime pay, but don't have the time or energy to have a life beyond their work. Anyone entering a particular field for the money and the lifestyle it affords is making a tremendous mistake. That "why" isn't strong enough to withstand the demands of the profession. Many new doctors finish medical school with six-figure loans to repay. Money alone will never be enough compensation for the commitment it requires. There never is a clear finishing point with money as a goal; you'll always want another comma in your check.

Realizing we're on the wrong track, even if we're not sure what the right one is, can be the first step toward making a life. In the church we use the word *repent*. The word applies in secular life as well. Turn around. Change course. Get back on the right track. Turn toward truth.

Mom's Corporate Detour

My mother had a similar revelation when she left the cosmetics company to take a great job with a financial services firm. Corporate life did not suit her, even when she succeeded in that world. She had some key skills for corporate success: people enjoyed working with her and wanted to follow her. But in the corporate world, Mom followed orders from those above her in the organization, and she was required to give orders to those below her—even if she disagreed with those orders. She lost the independence she had experienced building her own business with other independent businesspeople. She no longer felt like a part of her own team. She was an employee, and she was a boss.

GOD OPENS NEW DOORS

When I was still at Georgia Tech trying to figure out which direction to go, God showed me there would be other ways to serve—the "why" that He would speak to me—and over the next few years He began to open those doors. I attended First Baptist Church of Atlanta, just a few blocks from the Tech campus. They offered me the opportunity to work as assistant to the college pastor, and I was totally immersed in church again. I also met Lori Simril, who would become the love of my life.

I graduated from Georgia Tech in 1985 without a clue as to what to do with my career. Tech had prepared me for the business world, and I had job offers from IBM in Bowling Green, Kentucky; Proctor & Gamble in Green Bay, Wisconsin; and other corporations. But my heart, my family, my friends, my church, and my future wife were all in Atlanta, my hometown. So I stayed, and I followed the advice of an older friend to schedule appointments with thirty or so people I knew through my parents or who were parents of my high school and college friends—people who had been successful in business. They were giving me advice as if I were their son, and when I put all of their comments together, the consensus was a career in investments. Stocks and bonds. Insurance. Real estate.

I went to work with a man who made millions of dollars syndicating apartment complexes. He would bring together a group of investors to buy a property; they would all own a piece of the deal. It was a complicated business that relied on tax shelters and offered high-income investors incredible opportunities. And it was like a lion hunting elephants. My boss went out and made a tremendous deal and then lived on the proceeds until the next one.

I was twenty-two years old, and my boss said that after a couple of years I would learn enough to do what he did and earn what he earned. In the meantime, he paid me $17,000 a year while I worked and attended classes to earn my Certified Commercial Investment Member (CCIM) status. I sat at the table many times and watched him sign contracts that earned him hundreds of thousands of dollars. Other days I felt like I was just shuffling papers.

Lori and I married in July 1986, and then my job and my financial future got turned upside down. Congress passed the Tax Reform Act of 1986, which lowered tax rates and also eliminated the tax shelters my boss and his clients relied on, and almost overnight our office fell silent. All of the commission salesmen left, because there were no deals to be made. Nobody was buying.

By that time my boss had earned enough money to sit back, weather the storm, and figure out what to do next. My opportunity, on the other hand, had disappeared. I would have to manage on my base salary.

Lori was working as a legal assistant at a downtown Atlanta bank, so our combined income paid the bills, but that was not the life we envisioned. We were a little deeper in debt than we wanted to be. We were hoping to have children, and we wanted Lori to be able to stay at home. My income alone wouldn't allow that.

ROLE MODELS IN RON AND JUDY BLUE

When we married, Lori and I needed models for building a solid marriage and family. Lori's parents were a wonderful model for her growing up, but I never saw a healthy marriage close up.

Ron and Judy Blue became that model for us in our early years. Ron and Judy taught our Sunday school class, and in our first six months as a couple they taught us biblical principles of marriage. Ron was a CPA and financial planner, and he and Judy would soon write their first book together, *Money Matters for Parents and Their Kids*. Their biblical perspective on family and finances helped us clarify our priorities. Their message was: it's not how much you have, it's what you do with what you have. Having Ron and Judy as an example of a marriage built on godly principles was important to Lori and me getting off to a healthy start.

Ron gave us an image of stewardship that I have never forgotten. (He has since written seventeen books on personal finance from a biblical perspective.) He held his hands out, palms up, and said that God gives us everything we have. We all use different amounts of time, money, and resources. We can choose to hold these things with our palms open, which let's God know they are available to Him, or we can hold onto them ourselves. Ron closed his fists tightly to demonstrate.

The world wraps its hands around everything it can get, then holds on. But God owns it all, so He wants us to hold it in our hands loosely, then He can have access to it. Whatever He touches He will multiply—not always in the way we expect, but always in a way that brings joy.

WE CAN DO THIS!

Then one Sunday our pastor, Dr. Charles Stanley, who had married Lori and me, preached a sermon on the importance of getting out of debt. As a young couple, the world had taught us that debt was a natural part of life—something to live with. We were already in debt, so we didn't see any way to leave our jobs *and* pay back our credit cards.

What could we do? We had a hunger to resolve our problem.

One night we sat down to figure out how much money we actually needed. Lori was working in a downtown Atlanta bank, which meant she was paying for parking every day, gas for the commute, and maintaining a professional wardrobe, with dry cleaning bills that go along with that. If she left the bank, she could eliminate those expenses. We found other corners we could cut, and finally got to the bottom line: if she could generate $1,000 a month working from home, she could eliminate all those work-related expenses and replace her remaining income.

We didn't need to get rich—just generate $1,000 a month. We began to explore different industries, looking for one we believed in and that was on the upswing. What fields were experiencing growth that had not already peaked?

That's when Lori connected with a friend of a friend from church, Fran, whose husband, Ron, was an associate minister at a Presbyterian church. Fran had worked for Eastern Airlines for years, but had lost her job there (Eastern declared bankruptcy in 1989). She and Ron had to replace her income, so she joined National Safety Associates (now the Juice Plus Company), a company that relied on independent salespeople to sell water filters directly to customers. Fran was selling and also building a team of salespeople, whose sales would generate an additional stream of income for her. I had seen this model work with Mom's business!

Fran had a mercy personality type, and to me, at least, didn't seem like a person who could ever sell. Lori and I visited with her and her husband in her home, and she explained to us how she had built a small team to sell water filters, and each member of her team had built their own teams. In her first year her income had more than replaced her entire salary.

Driving home, I said to Lori, "If Fran can do that, we can do it. We only need $1,000 a month. We can make $1,000 a month, I guarantee."

The time seemed right for the product. There's a health crisis in this world, and people need to take control of their own health. Nothing is more appealing than our health. Everybody wants to feel better, look better, and live longer. Bottled water was expensive and hadn't taken the world the way it has in recent years, but people understood the importance of clean water, and they weren't sure what was going into their water upstream.

We also learned all we could about the company and liked what we saw. It was well managed and debt free. Our biggest concern was that the best way to start was with an investment of $5,000 for water filters we would sell. We didn't have that much money.

But the time and the economy were right for finding people to work with us. Some of the same economic changes that had led to Eastern's failure were having an impact in other industries. A lot of good people who had made a lot of money had the floor fall out from under them. People who had been earning six-figure incomes were making less than half that and were looking for new opportunities.

With so many things lining up for success, we went to the bank to see if we could borrow $5,000— they said they would give us a ninety-day note. Then we called Fran and said we would do it.

We were on our way.

You Know More People
Than You Realize

Lori and I looked at $5,000 worth of water filters stacked up in our garage and began to understand the term "buyer's remorse." They represented our first bank note ever—and we had ninety days to sell enough of them to pay back the loan.

I say "we," although Lori had taken on this challenge as her opportunity to build a business working from home. We were partners in every sense, but I was working full time in real estate. This was going to be her deal.

We had made our list of potential buyers starting with our family and working our way out from there—college roommates, church friends, neighbors, and so on. That process had been discouraging at first. Fran had said to make a list of 300 names, and after going through our wedding list, church directory, and high school yearbooks, we were stuck at 150.

We called Fran and told her our problem, and she said, "Pull out the Yellow Pages."

"You have got to be kidding," I said, thinking she meant for Lori to start making cold calls.

"No," she said. "You know so many more people than you think. Go through the Yellow Pages categories, and they'll remind you of who you know."

So we started with accountants and builders, and by the time we reached zoologists a few hours later, we had way more than 300 names. For example, when we saw "hardware," I remembered the Lawn-Boy mower I had bought as a teenager for my yard business, and wrote down the hardware store owner's name.

I didn't know the term *relational capital* at that point, but Lori and I felt the love of all those people even before she started making her calls. Lori's parents were the first to commit to her—not just to buy the product, but to become distributors themselves. They believed in the product and the company and their own ability to build a business. My mom bought one too and became a distributor, but she wasn't ready to leave her corporate career.

By the end of the first month we had thirty-eight customers and had paid back the loan. Lori earned her first check, and she resigned from her bank job.

Four months later I was able to leave my real estate job—an opportunity we had not anticipated. We saw a bigger vision and a bigger "why." All it would take was a commitment.

COMMITMENT

Did this ever happen to you when you were a kid?

You go to the store with your mom or dad and

buy a model airplane. You buy a tube of glue and bring it all home, then spread the pieces out all over the dinner table. You start matching pieces and gluing them together, but there are hundreds of them, and it takes longer than you anticipated. You don't work straight through—it's going to take several hours—and a couple of days later your mom asks you to clear the table. So you put all the pieces back in the box, then put the box on the top shelf in your closet so you can get back to it.

Three years later you're cleaning out the closet, and the model airplane pieces go into the garbage. You were not fully committed to building that model airplane.

Sometimes people need to risk so much they can't throw it into the garbage can. Remember the lesson of the explorer Captain Hernán Cortés, who ordered his men to burn the ships when they landed in Veracruz in 1519 so they wouldn't be tempted to turn back.

When Lori and I started our new venture, we couldn't walk away from a $5,000 loan. We were all in, like it or not.

Our business today requires only a $50 start-up investment, but those who succeed are the ones who are fully committed.

A Guarantee I Could Keep

When I got into the business, some people told me, "You're just going to make your friends mad when you ask all of them to buy stuff."

I said, "I guarantee you I'll have *more* friends because I'm in this business than if I were not. I'm not just asking them to buy stuff. I'm asking them to join me in a mission, and our company's mission: "To build a stable and lasting company that will help as many people as possible to realize their dreams."

We succeed when we pour into our friends, not when we take from them. In all our years in direct sales, we never asked anybody to buy something they didn't want. Instead, we asked if we could help them achieve their goals. How could they benefit?

It's all a matter of how well you steward your relationships. When we care about each other, we can do more together than we can alone.

Selling the Positive

The water filters we sold were like small kitchen appliances. I spent countless hours underneath kitchen sinks across north Georgia installing the filters, happy for every opportunity, and often humming the old Western song "Cool Water." All of our audio marketing material included Rex Allen, the singing cowboy, crooning, "cool, clear water."

We were selling water filters by reminding potential customers about the carcinogens and contaminants flowing out of their kitchen faucets. Often the conversation turned negative and even fear-based.

Then Jay Martin, president of the company, insisted that we emphasize a positive message rather than focusing on the fear of foul water from the tap. He said if people would just taste our filtered water— make a cup of coffee with this good water every day for a week—they would never want to go back. Yes, it's safer, but more important, it's better.

Yes, the water was safer and healthier, but what people responded to was the fact that it was *better*. We would install a filter and call back in five days to ask, "How was your coffee this week?"

Jay's emphasis on quality would continue with every product the company introduced. That quality would become a launching pad for future growth. And his concept of the "virtual franchise," which combines elements of franchising, direct sales, network marketing, and corporate America, would create opportunities for new generations who join the mission with a ground-floor chance to introduce the products to their unique markets.

MAKE A LIFE RIGHT NOW!

Work as hard as you can to build your nest egg during your prime years of your life, the world tells you, and then you can do unbelievable things when you retire.

That's the *worst advice ever*.

There's nothing wrong with saving for the future, but why spend thirty-five years making a living, with the hope of someday enjoying the fruits of your labor?

Make a life right now.

Live your life fully today.

Live out your purpose.

I'm not talking about money, cars, and houses. I'm talking about the ability to make the life you desire right now. To live with joy. To experience peace. To pursue the life you want with energy and zeal today— way more than just making a living.

FILL THE CHAIRS

Kerry Daigle is a boxing promoter from Louisiana who also was building a virtual franchise with our company about the same time Lori and I were getting started. "The number one thing you do," Kerry told me, "is put butts in chairs."

Then he told a story about a big boxing match in Mexico. The champion had been guaranteed a fee, the contender had been guaranteed a fee, and a prize would go to the winner. To generate that much revenue, the boxing ring had to be set up in a bullfighting stadium.

The event sold out, with more than 100,000 people watching.

Kerry finished his story, then asked me, "Who made the most money?"

"The winner, I guess," I said.

"Nope," Kerry said. "The champion got paid, but Don King, the promoter of the fight, made the most money. He's the guy who got all those people into the seats."

Kerry taught me the value and skill of promoting an event. I never promoted a boxing match, but I learned how to attract people to learn about our mission.

Hard Work and a Little Luck

My first business trip to Mexico had come together perfectly, with contacts in Mexico City who were ready and waiting to sell our products. Like so many business opportunities, this one had started through a series of coincidences: I had given a videotape to a friend who had family in Baton Rouge, home of Louisiana State University. LSU was a big banking college, and my friend had given the video to her dad, who had left it on the front seat of his truck. Over the summer their family had a bank intern visiting from Mexico and staying in their home. The young man watched the video and thought his father, who was a bank president back home, would be interested, so they called me.

It was 1993, before we were using the Internet and e-mail, so I made a lot of phone calls and sent dozens of faxes to find out whether my new friends wanted to engage at a deeper level. Another connection introduced me to a veterinarian who bred bulls for fight-

✦ ✦ ✦

If you don't have energy to play your game,

you're playing the wrong game. Change

games. The results may not happen imme-

diately, but if it's God's game, you're going

to feel a power surge, a resiliency, and ask,

"Why didn't I do this five years ago?"

✦ ✦ ✦

ing in Mexico. The two of them committed to bringing a dozen of their friends each to a meeting. Along the way I learned that Bob Burdick, a leader with our company from North Georgia, was also developing contacts in Mexico. We connected and decided to coordinate a trip together.

Bob is seventeen years older than I am and comes from a very different background. Bob dropped out of school to work full time painting water towers and radio towers for sixty-eight dollars a week in 1963. Then he was drafted, and after Vietnam met his future wife, Sue, while he was riding with his motorcycle friends. Seven years later they had five sons. He was hanging drywall for a living, and living in a rented house.

In 1987, two friends who were with our company told Sue they were concerned about her family's financial future, and they offered an opportunity to change directions. Sue told Bob, who was skeptical of any "scheme" that didn't involve physical labor. They agreed, however, that Sue would meet with the men, with the intention of rejecting their proposal. But when Sue heard the presentation and analyzed the numbers, she saw a way to supplement Bob's income and provide some extras for their children. Before long Sue was doing so well, Bob joined her in the business full time.

Six years later I was still a baby-faced, twenty-seven-year-old kid hoping to match Bob's work ethic and success with my enthusiasm. The day of my departure, traffic slowed as I drove to the airport, and I realized I was going to have to park in the hourly lot if I was going to make my flight. Twenty-four dollars a day. I wheeled up to the curb by Delta ticketing, totally stressed, and told an officer standing there, "Let me just run in and check my bag, and I'll be right back. I'm about to miss my flight."

"Okay," he said—this was 1993, a different time of security at the airport—so I grabbed my bag and ran into the terminal, where the line was a mile long. I had never been so nervous. I had to get on that plane. My new friends would lose all confidence in me if I couldn't even get to Mexico City. I pulled out my passport and my ticket and held them as one passenger after another slowly moved forward. Finally, it was my turn.

"Am I going to make my flight?" I asked the woman behind the counter.

"Yes," she said as she pulled a tag for my bag, "if you hurry."

Then she handed me my baggage claim ticket and I bolted for the gate, running down the escalator, through the moving sidewalk, and up the escalator

47

to the concourse and my gate just as the plane was boarding.

There's no relief quite like finding your seat on the plane and turning your destiny over to the pilot. Now he was in charge of getting us to Mexico.

At our first meeting, Bob and I immediately saw the potential for markets in Mexico City, Guadalajara, and Monterey. I didn't speak a word of Spanish, but I could read the excitement on the faces in the room. Our hosts spoke English and translated for us as Bob and I helped them cast a vision for them to join us on our mission in Mexico. We spent a week in the country, and almost every meeting went as well as the first one.

Packing my bag at the hotel, I was relaxed and pleased with our success . . . until I started looking for my car keys. Then it hit me—*my Jeep!* I never moved it from the curb back in Atlanta. I ran over to the phone and asked the operator, who thankfully spoke English, to help me find the phone number for the Atlanta airport and to place the call.

The phone rang, and I knew the answer to my question before I spoke it. Still, I had to ask.

"Can you look out the window and see if my Jeep Cherokee is outside?" I said. "I left it right there by Delta ticketing. It's in front of where you drop off your luggage."

"When did you leave it?" the woman asked.

"About ten days ago," I answered.

She gave either a little sigh or maybe a chuckle; it was hard to tell over the phone I was calling from in Mexico. But I didn't think she was looking out the window for my Jeep.

"I can assure you, sir," she said, "your car is not there. You'll have to call the City of Atlanta police."

"Where do you think it is?" I asked.

"They have an impound lot somewhere," she said, "but I don't know where."

We landed in Atlanta, and I didn't want to wake Lori and tell her what had happened, so I called George, my accountability partner, and asked him to pick me up. While he was on the way I called the Atlanta police. They told me my Jeep was in a lot close to downtown. George drove me to the address and pulled up next to a chain-link fence. A couple of Rottweilers ran up to the fence barking like crazy until a man hollered at them to back off.

"Can I help you?" the man asked.

I told him my car was impounded and I needed to get it out. He verified who I was and told me I'd have to pay seventy-five dollars to get it out.

I paid him and he gave me my keys, and as he closed the gate behind me, I started multiplying twenty-four dollars a day times my entire stay in Mexico. Turned out I had saved a lot of money leaving my car at the curb. It wasn't exactly valet parking, but I had saved over a hundred dollars.

Sometimes you work hard. Sometimes you are blessed. Sometimes you get lucky.

WILLING TO DO WHAT IT TAKES

After being introduced to the business by Fran and then working on deals in Mexico alongside Bob Burdick, I realized I'd be hard pressed to find two people more different than Fran and Bob. Fran was a quiet, unassuming airline ticket agent who conveyed care for others. Bob was a rural drywall hanger with an incredible work ethic, standing in front of a roomful of people explaining the financial model.

I learned that it wasn't education or experience that would determine success. It was a willingness to do what it takes to get there, and that's different for every person.

In our business you need to build a team of five leaders. Some people have the credibility to make six phone calls and find their five. Others have to have enough tenacity to make 100 phone calls to find their five.

So you can't say that the activity is the same for

every person, because everybody's level of relational capital is different.

When we were starting, the economy had turned sour, much like the recent recession. A lot of good people who were used to six-figure incomes were suddenly making $30,000 a year or less, or scrambling to make anything at all. They were looking for a way out and to do something else. A lot of white-collar, middle-management, middle-America people—great people—needed something else. Timing for that was good for us, and in thirty days, after hundreds of conversations, we had recruited five people to join our team.

Here's the next lesson we learned: the people you recruit don't always end up being the superstars, because people either can be a doer or a connector. We did have future superstars in our first five, but others connected us to the superstars who drove our business.

TWO
KAIROS MOMENTS

SECONDS, MINUTES, hours, days . . . life happens from birth to death.

Then, in an instant, something breaks through and changes everything. A child is born. A doctor says, "Cancer." In that moment time seems to slow down, or even stop, as the impact of the event sinks in. God lifts you out of your rut in an instant.

Other breakthrough moments are less dramatic but still transformative. Flashing blue lights appear in the rearview mirror. You're offered a business opportunity. A friend invites you on a mission trip.

These can all be kairos moments.

The Greeks had two words for time: *chronos* and *kairos*. The English word *chronology* obviously has its root in chronos, which is defined as a succession of moments. Tick-tock, tick-tock. Kairos, on the other hand, means the right time, an opportune moment, or even the supreme moment. A kairos moment is fleeting. Miss it, and it may never return.

The Greek god Kairos is shown with wings on his feet and a long shock of hair hanging down over his face, and as he comes toward you, you can easily grab on to that hair. But after he passes, the back of his head is bald. The fleeting opportunity is gone, and there is no way to get it back.

Kairos moments happen every day, when God breaks through with a *boom!* He drops a relationship, an event, a crisis, a business opportunity, a victory in your life. Suddenly you have a chance to take action (see graphic on next page). I strongly advise you to observe your circumstances and reflect on the event in your quiet time and in prayer. Scripture may also help put the moment into context.

Discuss the event and its meaning with someone you consider wise and can hold you accountable. Then repent. You may think that's an exclusively religious word, but *repent* simply means, "I'm going in the wrong direction, and I need to turn to go in the right direction—from making a living to making a life."

 When you decide you must act, then you need someone who will hold you accountable to your decision, and you need a plan.

You must believe in the plan, and you need partners who believe in you. The appropriate response

KAIROS MOMENT

to a kairos moment almost always includes change. Sometimes difficult change. Surround yourself with people who will support you in your new direction.

BEGIN WITH DISCOVERY

Making a life begins with discovery. We start living when we discover the life God has called us to. That discovery, and the pursuit that follows, is the ultimate pleasure—the deepest gratification a person can experience. If you're pursuing what you're passionate about because it's the way God's wired you, then you're going to be the happiest you've ever been.

When I was a teenager, our youth pastor told us that some people have to get hit with a hammer to get God's message. "But God loves you enough," he said, "that He'll use a sledgehammer if He needs to."

From that point forward, I began to pray, "God, I

want to be on Your course for my life, and I want to be in tune where I can hear You. Please help me to hear You, so that I'll respond when you use a tack hammer and not wait until You have to use a sledgehammer."

I'm not saying the prayer always works and you'll always get the tack hammer, but I do believe His still, quiet voice will speak to us in our morning quiet time, or in the Word, or through godly relationships around us. I believe we can pursue and listen to or hear God to the degree that we feel the tack hammer.

Whether sledgehammer or tack hammer, kairos moments can change our direction toward truth.

If you're like most people, the majority of your daily allotment of chronos time is spent sleeping and working. Both are important, especially six to eight hours of good sleep per day. The forty to sixty hours we spend working each week can complement our life, or it can be in constant competition with the life we want to make. The work we choose should provide sanity and a path to our purpose.

Let me explain this a bit more. If you spend forty to sixty hours each week in a job that keeps you from the life you want to make, and it's merely a huge amount of time invested in a paycheck, you will experience conflict. We all want to make money and provide a lifestyle for our families, but when the paycheck itself is the only goal, the victory can be empty. God designed and wired you to do great things. We are all at our happiest and we thrive when we are in pursuit of those great things. Your work may already be a catalyst toward that end. Or it could be the impediment that's keeping you from having any time or resources to head in that direction.

I "go to work" (actually, that means my basement if I'm not meeting with people) fired up because my business is on a mission, and I get to work with awesome people around the world. Not every day is perfect, but it's a relief to know that my work doesn't require me to trade hours for dollars. It's also become a platform for ministry, enjoying family, building relationships, starting new ventures, and seizing Kingdom opportunities.

My first job, just one year out of school, required a one-hour (sometimes longer) commute twice per day. It was actually making me crazy. I was beginning to understand and justify road rage. I was throwing away ten hours every week. They were used up. Consumed. And that didn't even include the mental and physical toll of the stress from battling traffic. I was even spending time daily plotting which route might be the least congested to go to and from work. Looking back on that waste of chronos time, I see the very

✝ ✝ ✝

As long as you're operating on your plan,

you can keep trying to plug in to God's

power, but you're going to blow a fuse

every time.

Once you plug in and say, "God, all I want

is what You want. I want to be on the path

that You want me to be on," you may learn

that God wants you in the woods

in a one-room shack.

But that's okay, because that's where your

greatest joy is going to be.

✝ ✝ ✝

definition of insanity, but I kept doing it with no option in sight.

Then I experienced a kairos moment that changed everything when our friend Fran showed Lori and me how we could build a business. Sitting in her living room listening to her explain the business model, my mind raced ahead to a future connected with people. It was an opportunity, a kairos moment, that we would not miss.

"You Can Be What You Want to Be"

A couple of kairos moments completely changed the course of my friend Kerry Daigle's life.

You can still hear the pain when Kerry remembers meeting with his high school guidance counselor. Kerry had been brought up by his grandparents in the poorest city in the poorest parish in the second poorest state in the nation. His Maw-Maw and Paw-Paw Daigle had given him everything they could, which wasn't much monetarily. They lived in a shotgun house with no hot water and no television. His grandparents spoke no English, only French. And they couldn't read in any language.

But Kerry had read about a boxer who had gone to New Orleans, 140 miles away, and he wanted to go there too—to the city. Maybe further. He thought boxing might be his ticket. So one summer as a teen-ager he got a ride from Opelousas to New Orleans, where he spent a week sleeping on the floor of a boxing gym just to learn about the sport. One day a big black limousine rolled up to the front door, and two men stepped out wearing fine Italian suits and ties, and shoes that Kerry thought must have cost more than his grandparents' house. Kerry turned to another guy in the gym and asked, "Who are those men?"

"They're boxing promoters," came the answer.

"I want to be a boxing promoter," Kerry said, and he began to ask more questions. Boxing promoters, he learned, take on financial responsibility for a fight. They pay for everything, from renting the arena to paying the fighters. Then they promote the fight—they put customers in seats. And at the end of the day they receive the profit (or repay the loss).

Kerry knew he could put customers in seats. Even as a teenager he could promote. So he went back home with a dream.

A few weeks later his high school guidance coun-selor was meeting with students to ask them about their plans for college and careers. Kerry sat across the desk from her and said, "I want to be a boxing promoter."

That was probably the first time the counselor had heard that answer. It was a dream too high for a poor kid like Kerry, and she decided to level with him.

"Kerry, I know your grandparents," she said. "I know where you live. You're not going to college. The best thing you can do is get a job and give back to your grandparents what they've given to you."

She broke his heart. Kerry knew she was right about one thing—he owed everything to his Maw-Maw and Paw-Paw. Maw-Maw had been ironing clothes for five cents a piece to help Paw-Paw pay the bills for as long as he could remember. How could he consider leaving to become a boxing promoter, of all things?

He trudged home, wiping away tears, his dream stolen. Maw-Maw saw him come in the door and insisted he tell her what was wrong. When he explained why he couldn't be a boxing promoter, Maw-Maw put her hand on his shoulder and looked him in the eye, all ninety-five pounds of her, and said, "You always told me you wanted your own business. That lady cannot tell you how to be a successful boxing promoter."

Then she said, "You can be what you want to be. I believe in you. You be a boxing promoter."

Breakthrough!

So at the age of eighteen, Kerry started promoting amateur boxing matches and bartending at night. Three years later he was promoting professional matches, and at age twenty-two he promoted his first nationally televised fight. Over the years he would work with every major boxing promoter and every major television network.

✛ ✛ ✛

Pursue the life God has for you. If you never do anything else, pause for a moment and make sure you're doing that.

✛ ✛ ✛

WORLD-CHANGING KAIROS MOMENT

My friend Tim Blank's kairos moment opened a new world of gardening for the twenty-first century with the design of the Tower Garden by Juice Plus.

My memories of gardening recall humid southern mornings as a child with my grandmother in her garden reaching into scratchy, sticky bean plants or pulling okra pods while the plants touched me with

61

their tiny spines—and slapping mosquitoes.

Even when I saw my first Tower Garden, which was billed as a convenient way to grow your own fruits and vegetables, I wasn't sure I wanted to do my own growing.

Then I brought one home, and one night a few weeks later Lori picked a salad for our dinner. It was nothing but cool. Major *wow*.

Lori showed off the Tower Garden, which was covered with huge plants by then, on Facebook, and several women at church saw it and ordered their own. More early adopters, with the first ones on their block.

A few years later, I now have a friend in Cumming, Georgia, who uses Tower Gardens to grow seedlings and produce for restaurants with high-quality, farm-to-table menus. On weekends he conducts grow-your-own food workshops. Another friend in Soperton, Georgia, grows thousands of heads of lettuce every month with his 300 Tower Gardens. In California, a hotbed of early adopters, Tower Gardens are popping up on patios and decks, on rooftops, and in restaurant parking lots, where chefs can pick fresh produce every day. Because the process uses 90 percent less water than a traditional garden, it's perfect in California during their historic drought, or even in the Arizona desert. And they work indoors with grow lights, providing year-round production.

✝ ✝ ✝

Kairos moments allow you to leave

the average and go to a level of greatness.

✝ ✝ ✝

Tim's kairos moment occurred when he was already living his dream. From 1993 to 2005 he worked at Epcot Center in Walt Disney World and traveled the United States and the world to confer with leading scientists about his work. He even collaborated with NASA, and more times than not his colleagues were seeking *his* advice.

Tim was chief horticulturist and manager of The Land Pavilion at Epcot, overseeing the science of hydroponic biomes. These were George Jetson gardens—way beyond cutting edge—and scientists and growers in the real world were drawn to the technology. This was exactly what Mr. Disney had in mind.

Walt Disney had presented his idea of Epcot, the Experimental Prototype Community of Tomorrow, in

1966, before Tim was born. Mr. Disney envisioned a place "like the city of tomorrow ought to be." A part of that vision included futuristic technology for growing high-quality, nutritious food.

Epcot opened in 1982, and Tim's father, a journalist and newspaper publisher, flew his family from Williston, North Dakota, to see it. At Epcot they took the "Behind the Seeds" tour of the hydroponic greenhouses in The Land Pavilion, and a new vision was planted in the head of seventeen-year-old Tim that would have the potential to change the world.

Tim grew up in Williston, sixty miles south of the Canadian border and twenty miles east of Montana, two thousand miles and a world away from Disney World in Orlando, Florida. Williston ran on agriculture and oil, two boom-and-bust industries that rode the roller coaster throughout Tim's childhood.

"Farming didn't bring in any real money," he says. "It just kept people there. But with an oil boom the city might grow from 10,000 to 20,000 in a matter of months, or shrink back just as fast with a bust."

During Tim's early childhood, his dad wrote for the local newspaper and lost his job in the midst of an oil bust. For nine months, until Mr. Blank could get his own publication up and running, church friends brought food to the family. "As a child in that situa-

✝ ✝ ✝

God cares so much that He constantly wants

to dive into chronos time and let us

experience a kairos moment with Him.

He says, "Look! I have more for you.

I have abundant life."

✝ ✝ ✝

tion, you understand what it's like to be on the fringe of nothing," Tim recalls. "I had two amazing parents who were willing to work hard in a place where opportunity didn't exist. That teaches you as a young guy the seriousness of life, of surviving."

Then changes in Washington, D.C., altered the economics of farming, favoring corporations over small farms.

"The small family farms started dying because farmers couldn't compete with big agriculture companies," Tim says. "The focus was on bigger farms and cheaper commodities. Most of the small farmers around us could tell us, 'My great-great grandfather broke this land.' But they couldn't afford to stay any longer. They were losing their livelihood, and some of them responded by turning to alcohol abuse, drug abuse, sexual abuse, and physical abuse. I saw girls come to school with bruises from their drunken fathers, and I began to feel like I had to help find a solution."

Tim also saw the impact of big agriculture on the land when he walked through the fields near his home. "I watched the aerial application of chemicals, and when I would cut through the fields later, I would see dead rodents and birds—not just insects. I didn't know what the chemicals were, but it didn't make sense to me."

GROWING LIKE THE FUTURE TODAY

The Behind the Seeds tour revealed a whole new world of agriculture for Tim—like nothing he had imagined in the fields back North Dakota. He gaped at the gleaming white maze of pipes and columns with perfect green vegetables bursting from them. Today someone might say the greenhouse looked like it had been designed by Steve Jobs for Apple. The lines were that clean and elegant. In the controlled-environment greenhouse, plants grew without soil, receiving the perfect amount of nutrients and minerals in water applied directly to their roots through the pipes.

"Instead of chemicals to control bugs, they used bugs to control bugs," Tim recalls. "It was a controlled-environment greenhouse—the solution to the unpredictability of farming."

Tim earned his college degree in horticulture and greenhouse management, but nothing he learned in college approached what he had seen at The Land. He wanted to go back there. So he applied for a six-month advanced internship after graduation and was accepted. He was going back to the future of farming.

"My goal for my internship," Tim says, "was to learn everything I could from the best hydroponic institution anywhere—learn all the things I didn't learn in college. And when my time was up there, I would start my own hydroponic farm."

Tim's goal became a driving force for his short six months at Disney. While the other interns socialized or enjoyed the Disney World parks after work, Tim stayed in The Land, working sixty- and eighty-hour weeks with the PhDs who were leading the research.

The scientists noticed Tim's commitment, and at the end of his internship offered him a one-year research project—and time to learn even more before starting his own farm. Another year-long project followed, then another. Tim studied plant nutrition, entomology, and the impact of LED lighting on plants for NASA, and much more.

"One project would end, and another would open," he says, "and I kept learning. If you have a purpose, a passion, and integrity, the Lord will present space for things to happen. I can only take credit for hard work, not for what the good Lord blessed me with."

After six years of research projects, Tim had doctoral experience in every horticultural discipline in the soil-less environment. Then in 2000, for the first time since The Land Pavilion had been created, the position of chief horticulturist and greenhouse manager became open. Tim was selected to oversee the system that had inspired him as a boy.

All along the way Tim and other scientists and interns were leading tour groups Behind the Seeds—like the tour his family had taken years earlier.

Every tour was different, because they were not tightly scripted. And the environment changed as plants grew and were harvested to be served in restaurants in Epcot. "Nothing was animatronic," Tim says. "We were literally growing food. It's the number one most repeated tour at Epcot."

At the end of almost every tour, whether he was

leading movie stars, governors, scientists, moms, dads, farmers, or children through The Land, Tim kept hearing variations of the same question: "How can I do this in my backyard?" "How can I do this on my farm?" "How can I do this for my farmers market stand?"

Visitors were inspired by what they had seen, and disappointed that when the tour was over, all Tim could do was point to a book in the lobby.

"I realized between 2000 and 2005 that the world needed us," he says. "No one was providing this incredible technology, this amazing research, to the world. It was part of the show at Disney, but it didn't seem to be making a difference outside."

That was Tim's next kairos moment.

A Passion for the Future

Tim began to consider where his passion for the future of gardening might intersect with the world's need for healthy food. Working in The Land had been a dream job, but it was no longer his passion. He still enjoyed collaborating with researchers, but now he wanted to share his knowledge with a world that hungered for nutritious, pesticide-free, easily accessible fresh food.

Continuous change and significant transitions have always been part of Tim's life. "I could not imagine doing the same thing for the rest of my life," he says. "I'm always yearning to becoming more than I am now." He adds that he had a personal mantra similar to a statement Steve Jobs made in his 2005 Stanford University commencement address:

"I have looked in the mirror every morning and asked myself: 'If today were the last day of my life, would I want to do what I am about to do today?' And whenever the answer has been 'No' for too many days in a row, I know I need to change something."

"I was thinking of leaving and starting a company," Tim says, "but I was just twelve years away from full retirement. Maybe I could do it then."

Then he met Jessica, who would become his wife, working at Disney. "Jessica's belief in me gave me encouragement," Tim says. "She reminded me that I had learned from the best of the best. She encouraged me to follow my passion to help people. And she said we could do it together.

"It was time," he says. "I didn't know what my company would be or how I would transition, but it was time to spread my wings."

Jessica's encouragement and Tim's decision to

leave the relative safety of the corporation remind me of the mother eagle pushing the baby off the edge of the nest to fly.

In 2005 Tim and his wife, Jessica, with the support of several other international hydroponics experts, founded a consulting company they called Future Growing LLC, with the goal of helping clients create and operate successful urban farms, often on rooftops, using the latest technology in hydroponics and aeroponics.

"We knew from the start," Tim says, "that we would be going vertical—like modern cities. Traditional greenhouses are enormous. Every decade since World War II they've gotten bigger and more expensive, and they're filled with a sea of green with everything growing just six inches tall. Commercial growers were not using vertical technology the way we had at Epcot."

Tim and Future Growing helped design and build the world's first certified "green" building, The Garden Building in Orlando, with a greenhouse on the roof filled with an aeroponic urban garden and a commercially scaled fish farm. Other projects followed, and at the same time Tim worked to develop a small-scale vertical hydroponic system for families and commercial production: the Tower Garden by Juice Plus.

Tim's kairos moments have revealed opportunities that have affected thousands of people and are literally changing our world.

KAIROS MOMENTS AND HEDONISM

The first time I heard the term "Christian hedonism," I thought somebody must have made a mistake. Hedonism is the pursuit of pleasure and self-gratification—just the opposite of what most people consider Christianity to be.

But John Piper's book *Desiring God* opened my eyes to the truth that the ultimate pursuit of pleasure is finding the life God has called me to live. God wants us to change our paradigm to: *God knows what's best for me. God wants the most joy for me. God wants the most abundance for me.*

Piper states it clearly in these two sentences:

"By Christian hedonism, we do not mean that our happiness is the highest good. We mean that pursuing the highest good will always result in our greatest happiness in the end."

So what is the "highest good"? God will break through into your chronos time with truth in a kairos moment—sometimes just an instant—and with the answer. In that instant, when time seems to stand still, He will reveal truth that can show the way to a life more fulfilling than you ever dreamed or imagined.

You are the created, and the Creator made everything, including you, for His own pleasure. He put you geographically where you are, connected you with the people around you, and gave you certain resources for reasons He will tell you. That's a promise. "He not only knows what He's thinking, but He lets *us* in on it. God offers a full report on the gifts of life and salvation that He is giving us. We don't have to rely on the world's guesses and opinions. We didn't learn this by reading books or going to school; we learned it from God, who taught us person-to-person" (1 Corinthians 2:11-13, MSG).

You Must Pursue Your Passion

If you choose a life that doesn't allow you to pursue your passion, it doesn't matter how much money you make, how hard you work, how many people you impress, or how many titles you get. Don't buy into the world's version of checking the boxes. God wired you to do more than check boxes. He gave you your own "why."

Of course, it's impossible to know exactly how tomorrow will look, but if you can discover what you *want* your tomorrow to be, and that place is awesome, then today you can plan and then take the first steps—take the first bite out of the elephant—to get there.

Your elephant might be as big as a job change, or it might simply be putting some boundaries up in your life and job. If you've been doing the same thing for years and you don't feel like you're any closer to "awesome" than when you started, then something needs to change. Our company's top earner, my dear friend Jeff Roberti, often reminds us of an old saying, "For things to change, *you've* got to change."

Tomorrow changes today.

You may be ignoring change. That seems like your course of least resistance. But at that rate, in five years you won't be any closer to awesome than you are today. Doing the same thing will get you the same results.

All you have to do today is start the process. Take a step. Take one step out of your comfort zone, and you're taking one step out of your rut. That's all. One step.

Kairos moments break through more often when you're *un*comfortable.

This message of "make a life, not just a living" begins to make sense when you respond to the revelations in your kairos moments.

Pursue your passion—the thing you're good at and are equipped to do—and you're going to be the happiest you've ever been.

THREE
FIND YOUR PURPOSE

WHEN I WAS A TEENAGER, twenty years before Rick Warren published his mega-best-selling book on the subject, my friend and mentor Gary O'Malley was urging me to seek God's purpose for my life—to complete the sentence, "I exist to _____."

Kevin McCarthy's book *The On-Purpose Person* had resonated with Gary, and he wanted me to tap into my highest potential. I would have to grow and experience more of life before I could answer Gary's challenge, but even then I knew that purpose, or lack of purpose, can dramatically determine the amount of zeal and vigor present for the day at hand as I pursue life. Today I can say that I exist to "make a life, not just a living." Within that statement I embrace the vision of the company I work for: "Inspiring healthy living around the world."

Discovering my purpose was not an event, but it is a process still going on today. Yes, I did learn and write a purpose statement, but it is ever evolving and being modified as life brings new environments, people, and changes to my life (i.e. marriage, children, moves, etc.).

Successful people are on some type of "mission." They live with purpose. They have either joined a mission that already exists or they have started one of their own. Those who haven't joined a mission can only contribute at a shallow level, without focus and impact. I'm grateful that people have cared enough about me and our mission to join us. That may be one of the most important aspects of making a life. You cannot do it alone.

I encourage you to develop a brief statement of purpose—to complete Gary's sentence, "I exist to _____." The statement should be uniquely yours, one you can live on purpose and with passion.

This isn't a project for an afternoon or even a weekend. Think about it. Pray about. Talk about it with the people who know you best. Read books like *The On-Purpose Person* and *The Purpose-Driven Life*. You are not deciding; you're *discovering* your purpose. Gary often reminded me, "No eye has seen, no ear has heard, no mind has conceived what God has prepared for those who love him—but God has revealed it to us by his Spirit." That truth was written by the Apostle

✠ ✠ ✠

You need to be on task with your mission

and purpose and passion so that when you

bump into somebody, you're contagious.

You're infecting them with your passion

about life so much that they need to call the

CDC because you're starting an epidemic.

✠ ✠ ✠

Paul to the church in Corinth, and it reminds me that God will reveal our purpose to us.

Once you discover your purpose and are able to articulate it to yourself and others, that statement will enhance your effectiveness and your ability to message and multiply your mission.

There's a story of a man who walks into a construction site and sees a guy working and sweating as he lays bricks. The bricklayer is fast and does good work, scooping mortar with his trowel, laying it on top of the wall, then pressing the next brick into place.

"What are you doing?" the visitor asks.

The bricklayer never takes his eye off the bricks—never looks at the visitor.

"Laying bricks," he says, then he scrapes the excess mortar and repeats, almost machinelike. The visitor moves on and lets him get back to his work.

Another worker around the corner appears to be doing the same thing—picking up bricks, scooping mortar, pressing bricks into place—and the visitor asks, "What are you doing?"

The bricklayer steps back and motions down the forty-foot-long wall that's now three feet high and growing. "I'm building a wall," he says with a note of pride.

"Looks nice," the visitor says. "Nice work."

"Thank you."

The visitor walks around the corner and a third worker is likewise scooping mortar, placing bricks, and scraping excess mortar.

"What are you doing?" the visitor asks.

The bricklayer puts down his trowel and motions for the visitor to step back from the work site. "We're building a cathedral," the worker says with a sweep of his hands. Then he describes the handcrafted doors and stained-glass windows that will be placed in the wall he's building, the spires and the steeple and the cross that are to come. "I pray with every brick I lay," he says, "for the people and families that will worship in this place."

Three men doing the exact same job. One understood why, and it made all the difference. Lori and I saw the cathedral, and that is when we knew we were no longer just selling, but building a business.

Why do you do what you do?

New Opportunities

When you're operating in alignment with your purpose, unexpected opportunities arise. In the late 1980s a friend invited Lori and me to the National Prayer Breakfast in Washington, D.C., where thousands of people gathered from around the globe at the intersection of the political, economic, and biblical worldviews. Everyone was made to feel comfortable; no one felt threatened. And as we watched all of these people talking with each other about their faith and their experiences, we thought we might try something similar at our company's upcoming gathering of leaders.

Several thousand people attended our four-day conference in 1989, and on Friday morning, seventy of us gathered for breakfast and listened to Don Kingsborough (former Atari executive who founded

✝ ✝ ✝

Instead of wondering how many followers

you have, shift your thinking to consider

how much influence you have. What are you

going to do with that influence?

✝ ✝ ✝

Worlds of Wonder, creator of Lazer Tag and Teddy Ruxpin, among others) talk about his journey of faith. Don's amazing story was life changing for many in the room.

Then three months before our next conference, I started getting calls and messages asking, "Where is the prayer breakfast? Who's going to speak this time?" We hadn't planned for a second one, but God almost forced us because of demand from believers in our business. We had done something that God obviously used in the lives of the people. So with very little time, I contacted another speaker, and since then the prayer breakfast has continued twice yearly, at every Juice Plus Conference, with two thousand to three thousand people attending—almost as many as the National Prayer Breakfast!

PURPOSE: DRILL BITS OR HOLES?

The guy at the hardware store thought he was being helpful by explaining the pros and cons of various drill bits. He had paddle bits and countersink bits, carbide-tipped bits and titanium-coated bits.

I never knew there were so many drill bits. All I wanted was to go home and finish building my deck. Our cabin in the woods was seventeen miles from the nearest store, and I had been working all morning setting posts. When I started attaching the joists, I realized my drill bit wasn't long enough. I couldn't drill a hole all the way through. So I had driven into town to the store. Now I was getting a life lesson on drill bits.

"I just need a quarter-inch hole in a six-by-six post," I interrupted.

"Oh, okay," he said, reaching for an eight-inch bit. "Here's what you need."

I thanked him and paid for my new drill bit, then I drove out of the parking lot with the realization that we sometimes get caught up in sharing our solutions before we've listened to the problem. We slap people over the head with the thing we think they need—

salvation tracts instead of sitting down with them, finding out where they're hurting, and sharing how God can fill the hurt in their life. Or we suggest a career change to join our mission before we've heard the whole story.

As it turns out, our business isn't the answer for everybody who has a financial problem. Some people need a different drill bit to make a different hole. Our role isn't to explain how every drill bit works, or how great our drill bit is, until we listen and hear what the other person needs. That's the skill I'm trying to learn, hearing the answer to, "What kind of hole do you need? Do I have the right drill bit to help?"

KEEP PUNCHING

Kerry Daigle knew that you can't run a boxing business without access to credit. The cash flow just doesn't work that way. In the early 1980s Kerry had a line of credit with a bank, and everything was working well. Then the FDIC shut down the banks, and in a matter of weeks, without access to that line of credit, Kerry could no longer borrow enough money to finance a fight.

"Some of that was my own fault," he says looking back, "but the only thing that mattered was that I lost everything. My business, my home—my self-confidence."

His grandparents had passed away by then, so there was no going home to Opelousas. A friend with a mobile home dealership let him live in one of his homes until he could get back on his feet. He rented a post office box, because he was embarrassed for people in the boxing business to send him mail at the mobile home park.

He always checked his mail in the middle of the afternoon when the post office was empty so he wouldn't run into anybody he knew. He felt like a laughingstock—like he had proven his high school guidance counselor right. He could no longer be a boxing promoter.

One afternoon in the post office he was peering into his little box and felt a hand on his shoulder. He turned and saw a familiar face.

"Kerry Daigle, where have you been?" the man asked.

"I've been out," he said vaguely. "Around." Then he added a few details that sounded good but might not have been completely true.

The man knew better. He looked at Kerry and said, "I want to tell you something. I understand what happened to you from a financial standpoint. But there is one thing they can't take away from you."

He paused, and Kerry didn't know what was

coming next. "Your still own your skills," the man said. "They can't take your skills from you."

Finding the Dream Again

Kerry walked back to his car thinking, *He's right. They took my money, but they didn't take my skills. I'm going to get better. I'm going to read, study, and do everything I can to be a better promoter.*

Without access to cash, he couldn't promote fights himself, so he contracted with other promoters, large and small, making matches and putting fighters together for a fee. All the while he read every personal development book he could find. He listened to tapes in the car and watched videos at home.

By 1989 he still didn't have enough cash in the bank or access to credit to promote his own fight, but he was loving being in the business.

At the same time a friend was asking Kerry to meet him to talk about a business opportunity. Kerry didn't want to say no, so he hid. "I'd run to the bathroom or jump in my car and take off if I saw him coming," Kerry says. "But he was a friend, so I knew I had to talk to him sometime."

Then he had a great idea: he would ask his friend to meet with his wife, Mickey. If she said no, Kerry was off the hook. If she said yes, he would help.

"Mickey sat with him for two hours," Kerry says, "and the next day she quit her job and started her own virtual franchise. Scared me to death! Then she sat me down and explained it to me."

"All your life, Kerry Daigle, you've said to follow people more successful than you are. Now, how long have you known Emile Steckler?"

"All my life," I said.

"Has he been successful?" (Emile lived in a beautiful antebellum house. He was a multi-millionaire.)

"Yes," I said.

"Are you a millionaire?"

"No."

"You teach this all the time. Make sure you have mentors more successful than you. So why not listen to him?"

Kerry shrank from six feet tall to feeling about four-feet-one, and he went back to his office with his ego in his back pocket.

"I was so busy trying to stay alive financially, I forgot what people had taught me," he says. "You have to have the right mentors. You can't have somebody making $30,000 teaching you to make $100,000."

The next day Kerry became Mickey's first distributor, and they went on to build a tremendously successful business.

RESPONDING TO GOD'S CALL TO SHINE LIGHT INTO DARKNESS

When Kathrine Lee tries to understand how God has revealed her purpose, she begins with the death of a thirty-one-year-old friend, Kelly, who, along with the child she was carrying, died of an aortic aneurysm. Driving home from the funeral, Kathrine cried out to a God she didn't believe in but remembered from her youth, "If You're real, prove it to me."

Kathrine had built an extremely successful business when, not long after Kelly's funeral, God broke her heart over the issue of sex trafficking of young women. Then He moved her to action. The call didn't come in an instant, but through a series of experiences over time, beginning with an encounter on an airplane.

We are surrounded in our world by unspeakable horrors. I believe God wants us to be aware and sensitive to these issues. I also believe He touches the hearts of some people in a special way, calling them to do something more.

Kathrine was tired and needed some quiet time, so she put on her headphones and opened her Bible in her lap. Her body language couldn't have been clearer: "Leave me alone."

But the man in the next seat tapped her on her shoulder anyway and asked a question. Kathrine lifted one earphone and looked, without actually turning her head, as if to say, "What do you want?" The man didn't get the message and tapped her shoulder again. Finally, on the third tap, Kathrine felt God urging her to talk to him. She responded with a silent, surly prayer, "Do I have to?"

As it turned out, the man was smart, charismatic, and charming, and Kathrine began thinking which of her single friends she might set him up with. Deep into their conversation, Kathrine asked the question many people ask first: "What do you do?"

He answered, "I own the second-largest pornography company in the world."

✝ ✝ ✝

The words shocked Kathrine,

but almost as quickly, she experienced

an unexplainable peace.

✝ ✝ ✝

The whole conversation had been a setup, an opportunity for the man to shock or embarrass her. He had seen Kathrine's Bible, and had led her along, knowing all the while that when she learned what he did, she would judge him and immediately reject him. He thought that would be funny. Kathrine realized all this in that split second between his answer and her response, and she knew just as clearly that this moment had been orchestrated not by the man sitting beside her but by God. She was determined to meet the man with love, grace, and curiosity, however frightening his answers might be.

Kathrine asked questions and learned that recruiters in the porn industry go to places where high school girls hang and look for girls who appear to have "daddy issues." The recruiters talk with them about opportunities in modeling, then slowly lead them in.

"I thought men were supposed to be protectors of women," Kathrine said. "At three in the morning, does your hero's heart ever rise up to protect women?"

The man talked about his family—his ex-wife and his daughter who lives with her.

"So your daughter has daddy issues," Kathrine said, and for the first time she saw a crack in the man's confidence. He apparently had not considered his

✝ ✝ ✝

Join a mission

where your purpose

and passion

can thrive.

✝ ✝ ✝

daughter as a target of his recruiters.

As their plane descended the man said, "I will never sleep the same again." Then he asked for Kathrine's business card. "Someday my daughter may need you." She didn't know yet what was behind that conversation, but an invitation to a Los Angeles ministry would make it clear.

Dream Center reaches out to people in need of food, shelter, rehabilitation, and much more. Kathrine visited a service there with a friend, and she felt led to ask the pastor's wife specifically what she and her husband, Michael, might pray for.

"Pray for Project Hope, our home for survivors of domestic human trafficking."

Kathrine instantly made the connection to her conversation on the airplane. "Caroline could have told me so many other things about Dream Center— their homeless shelter, their feeding ministry—but she named this one ministry—Project Hope and caring for those who rescue girls on front lines."

Kathrine began to research the issue, and she learned that sex trafficking was the second-largest and fastest-growing criminal industry in our country, and she believed they were being called to step in. Then she and Michael prayed to God, "You have blessed us. What do you want us to do with our blessings?"

✝ ✝ ✝

When you ask that question,

you'd better be prepared,

because God may reveal a purpose

for your life beyond anything

you dreamed you could handle.

✝ ✝ ✝

A third encounter took place when Kathrine was telling her own story in front of a group of people, and she discussed her growing realization of the emerging call for her and Michael. On the front row several young women began to cry. She spoke to them afterward, and they apologized, explaining that they were survivors of human trafficking. Now Kathrine was crying too. The call couldn't have been clearer if it had been chiseled in stone.

Kathrine and Michael have answered by selling their home in California and buying a place in East

Texas where they are creating a safe place for women escaping from trafficking.

She says that moment was pivotal in the trajectory to where her life is now.

Kathrine's middle name is Nadine, which she learned means *hope*, and Kathrine means *pure*. "Remember who you are," she felt God telling her in the days following Kelly's funeral. She began to make decisions based on her heart's desire, not on survival.

"All of us were designed from the beginning of time with a purpose in mind," she says.

"I was given the name Kathrine Nadine—pure hope. For the first time, I knew God had meant that name to be something special."

FOUR
GOD'S ABUNDANCE

MY FRIEND STEPHEN RITZ, who founded the Green Bronx Machine to teach at-risk inner-city kids, uses an age-old example that illustrates for me the meaning of abundance. Stephen shows his audience a glass of water and asks if it is half empty or half full. The answer, we've been trained to believe, reveals whether we are optimists or pessimists.

But Stephen says the glass is 100 percent full of water and air, two things we cannot live without. We must, he says, embrace a mind-set of endless resourcefulness. It's no wonder kids call him the Chief Eternal Optimist.

A life of abundance does not require a huge bank account, although material wealth might be part of an abundant life. I'm talking about living from an abundance mentality versus a scarcity mentality. Living in confidence instead of worry.

In my real estate job right out of college, I was

not a deal maker. For Lori and me, living abundantly would never mean a huge bank account. God knew that my faith was not strong enough to trust Him if I had the pot of gold sitting there. He lets some people build a stockpile because they manage that well, and they're different than I am. He blessed me instead with a business that provides reliable cash flow. I've never been able to create Fort Knox, so I've not replaced my faith in God with faith in my bank account. His cash flow is sufficient.

This is the heart of a life of abundance. God says, "I want you to pursue Me relentlessly. That's who I've wired you to be. We're going on a journey together, and I'm never going to let you arrive at a place where you can stop pursuing Me. But your pursuit will never be a burden. I've wired you that way—to pursue Me and to bring people with you on that pursuit."

HIGH TIDES AND LOW

One of our first really cool blessings and benefits of the business was the opportunity to buy a beach house at Fripp Island, South Carolina. We loved the sun rising out of the Atlantic Ocean and setting over the wide green marsh.

The water called out to us every day. I had been out on a boat before, when someone else drove the charter, and it was a fun way to explore the creeks and rivers that wind through the grassy marshes. So one weekend we rented a twenty-one-foot center-console flat-bottom boat for half a day. At midmorning we headed out from the marina just tooling around down to Pritchards Point, where we saw dolphins, and were having a great time—the kids, the dog, Lori, her sister, and me. We followed one creek that cut deep into the marsh, with waves of tall grass almost to the horizon. As I continued up the creek, I was careful to glance back to make sure I could see the Fripp Island bridge in the distance.

The tide was rising, lifting our boat higher in the creek as we tooled along. Then I looked back toward the bridge, and the grass was completely submerged. The creek had become part of the sea, all water, and I panicked. I couldn't see the channel at all. I glanced at the depth finder and pulled back on the throttle just as the propeller plowed mud, and I thought I had torn up the engine. I raised the engine a few inches then pushed the throttle gently. More mud. We were stuck. Within minutes the tide turned, and we were left sitting on a mudflat.

I called the marina and asked if they could come pull us out, and they said we would have to wait until the tide came all the way back in again late in the

✝ ✝ ✝

God says live life abundantly, but too many people do not acknowledge God when they're in the middle of abundance, because they don't need Him. They think they can handle life. Everything's going well. "I don't need God right now." We get away from God when things are going well, and then all of a sudden life spins out of control, and we cry out for Him. It's easy to wake up and have a quiet time when there's a crisis going on. Wake up and have a quiet time in the good times and let God fill your tank so you can be pouring out God that day instead of pouring out of yourself.

✝ ✝ ✝

afternoon. Our half-day on the water turned into a miserably hot August afternoon on the boat in the mud. We rationed our water bottles and nibbled our snacks as we watched the tide slowly recede all the way out and just as slowly return. Finally, sometime near sundown, we saw the towboat winding its way into the creek.

Writers have used the analogy of the tides to convey their meaning for centuries, but when I experienced the tide's impact firsthand, I had a better understanding of Shakespeare when he wrote in *Julius Caesar*:

> *There is a tide in the affairs of men.*
> *Which, taken at the flood, leads on*
>   *to fortune;*
> *Omitted, all the voyage of their life*
> *Is bound in shallows and in miseries.*
> *On such a full sea are we now afloat,*
> *And we must take the current*
>   *when it serves,*
> *Or lose our ventures.*

Shakespeare was writing about war, but the analogy holds for business too. Finding the high tide and harvesting in high tide with your bucket is the easiest way to make a life and build a business that supports the life you want to make.

The answer isn't always obvious. The day I took my family out in the boat, I saw a rising tide and rode with it. But I hadn't taken into account the fact that the tide was almost at its peak and would soon be flowing out.

Jesus told the crowd that before building a tower, you should first sit down and estimate the cost to see if you have enough money to complete it. When the tide looks like it's rising and the opportunity looks right for you, do your homework.

IDENTIFYING AND ANALYZING OPPORTUNITIES

The struggle for life and work balance is real. You see it every day if you participate in rush hour from your car. You see people leaving their homes before the first family conversation, and returning exhausted to eat and go to bed. We build a lifestyle and then we find a job to support it. The problem is our culture goes after the lifestyle instead of the life they desire.

Some people work in jobs that align with the life they desire to craft, but in most cases, our jobs keep us from that life. To bring this chaotic life to a place of a desirable life begins with a decision that the life

✝ ✝ ✝

My God is not

a Sunday God.

My God is

a 24/7 God.

He is in the details.

He is in the mundane.

✝ ✝ ✝

you desire is not connected to the number of hours you work.

You can make a life, instead of a living, when your work (what you are paid for) and your purpose (what you were created for) find each other. The way you generate income must become a foundation for the life you were created to live, not its competitor. In order to pursue your purpose with passion and live a life of abundance, you must stop trading hours for dollars. Please, don't wait until you retire! Most of your ability to live life to the plus is already gone at that point.

A subculture of financial advisors encourages you to work more so you can save more. "Build your nest egg so you can retire and enjoy the good life." Work like crazy and earn beaucoup of money for thirty years, and then you'll be able to retire and make a life. But you're killing yourself building this cash mountain before you can enjoy life.

Jesus tells a parable about a man who harvested so much grain, he tore down his barns and built bigger barns to store all of it. Then the man planned to retire to "eat, drink, and be merry." That very night he dropped dead, so he never enjoyed the bounty he had stored for later.

Why would you want to wait until you are in your

sixties to enjoy the good life? Or to create a life that matters? That would mean twenty to thirty years of rush-hour commutes. There is another option.

Robert Kiyosaki has written several books talking about the "cash flow quadrant." His model shows four possibilities of income/finance that could emerge:

Employee | Business Owner

You Have A Job
TIME = $

You Own A System &
People Work For You
PEOPLE = $$$

NO LEVERAGE   E | B   LEVERAGE
NO LEVERAGE   S | I   PASSIVE INCOME

You **OWN** A Job
TIME = $$

Money Works For You
$$$ = $$$$$$

Self-Employed | Investor

The first two of these models in the "cash flow quadrant" show that we are most concerned about "security," and the latter two show our motivation is "freedom." You may think the self-employed and business owner are the same, but the big difference is that the employee and self-employed (retail owner, doctor, lawyer, accountant, etc.) all trade the investment of the hours they have for dollars (I call it trading hours for dollars). The business owner has built a business that pays them because the system they have built generates income, and the investment of additional hours is not required to generate additional income. The investor (at least in stable markets) has accumulated or inherited wealth that produces his income.

If you live on the security side, you go to work (investing your hours) to generate income. The problem with this is the statistics showing how many people don't like their work, don't like being around the people they have to work with, and still invest the majority of their lives there.

The key here is finding an opportunity that allows you the ability to see light at the end of that tunnel— the light of abundant living. Can you see investing yourself into an opportunity that someday will no longer require you to make it happen each and every day, yet still produce the income?

In Kiyosaki's cash-flow quadrant, that opportunity is the business owner. You have a choice to own a business that allows you to stop being the "hands on the steering wheel." Think about a taxi driver. His income grinds to a complete halt the minute he doesn't sit behind the wheel. A surgeon, when not in the operating room, isn't making any money.

You can build a business that generates income without having to invest all of yourself all of the time.

WORK NOW, MISSION LATER? MAYBE NOT

Many books have been written about people who work in their jobs today, then do something "significant" when they've laid aside enough money. Bob Buford's book *Halftime* is one of the best on this subject. Unlike the man in the parable who built bigger barns for himself, they believe they're building bigger barns for someone else . . . someday.

Early in life they say, "God, I'll take care of the job part. I don't need You for that. I've got my degree, and I'm going to go get my job, and make the money I need. Then after that, God, it's me and You. We're going to do ministry over here."

They compartmentalize. But their lifestyle gets to a point where making a living takes up too much room, and there's only a little bit left for making a life. The outcome is the same as the man who builds barns for himself.

We need to learn to make a life *while* we're making a living, not make a life *after* we've made a living. Love what you're doing, and do what you love—what you're good at it. Let that create the life that you want to have right now.

I really believe that if you make yourself available to do what God's called you to do, He's also going to open the right doors for you to generate the income you need.

LIVE LIKE YOU'RE ON VACATION

Wendy Campbell understands living a life of abundance as well as almost anyone I know. Her idea of abundance had nothing to do with money. Wendy was just eighteen years old, a brand-new high school graduate, on her first day in beautiful Waikiki walking down Kalakaua Avenue along the beach among crowds of tourists, soaking in the sunshine. She had moved from Southern California to Hawaii, by herself, didn't know a soul, with dreams of eventually attending the University of Hawaii School of Nursing once she had fulfilled the two-year requirement for residency.

"I had wanted to be a nurse ever since I read the Cherry Ames Student Nurse books as a young girl," she says. And she was totally on her own. Her father, a wealthy and successful general contractor, had divorced her mom when Wendy was ten years old, did not support the family well, and basically told her she would have to finance her own college education. That was fine with her.

Wendy had made one decision long before leaving home. "I wanted adventure," she says. "Not a career to make money. In fact, because my dad was alcoholic and our family very dysfunctional, I linked money with pain and determined if I were going to set any goal at all, it would be not to make money. I saw hurt and manipulation and everything else negative associated with wealth; certainly nothing positive."

She made another important decision during her first day walking among those tourists. She observed that most of them were much older than she. Many were using canes and walkers to get around, and they didn't look particularly happy. They might have worked uninspiring jobs trading time for dollars; saved money their entire lives to get a week or two of vacation time in Hawaii, she thought, and then they would be going back to their regular lives.

Wendy was not "going back." That was not the life she wanted. Right then, right there, she pledged silently, "I'm going to live every day as if I'm on vacation."

Her vacation mind-set didn't mean she wouldn't work, but that she would enjoy her work. She didn't realize her decision would lead to occasional weeks when she had to live on pancake mix and water or sometimes wonder where the rent money would be coming from, but she did finish nursing school and built a nursing career serving others with joy in a variety of health care arenas.

Two decades later Wendy was living in St. Louis where her husband's job as a corporate executive had landed them. She was forty-three years old with children six, ten, and eleven, and married to Jim, whom she had met and married in Hawaii. "My husband is an angel," she says, but she didn't feel well adapted to being a housewife, conforming to the expectations for a corporate wife with rules about what you wore for different functions, the house you lived in, and the cars you drove. She didn't feel she fit into the mold and probably didn't enhance his career much either. She went on to say, "I loved volunteering at the kids' school and was looking to a different nursing arena, maybe hospice, but in many ways it felt like the vacation was over. I felt guilty at times because I was so blessed with my sweet husband and family, but I still felt that there were more mountains to climb."

A Skeptical Listener

Wendy listened politely, but was skeptical as a neighbor told her about Juice Plus, fruits and vegetables in a capsule. "I was a nurse," she says. "I wanted to see research and documentation, and at that time there was very little."

Then the cover of *Newsweek* magazine, April 25, 1994, changed her life:

The Search for the Magic Pill.
Better Than Vitamins.
Can "Phytochemicals" Prevent Cancer?
The Truth About Antioxidants.

Wendy dug into the article and learned that phytochemicals, which only occur in plant foods, were the "new frontier in health research," and had important anticancer benefits. "In the world where science merges with health, phytochemicals are the next big thing," *Newsweek* wrote. "The National Cancer Institute is so excited it has launched a multimillion-dollar project to find, isolate and study them. Private firms are eyeing them as a health blockbuster."

Wendy looked around and recognized that children were getting diseases that only old people got when she had started her nursing career. "When I was supervisor of a clinic in Hawaii," she says, "I didn't take care of one diabetic child. Now it's epidemic. I cared for just one child with cancer; now there are whole hospitals for pediatric cancer patients."

The *Newsweek* article sparked passion in Wendy.

"I was raised in the Sixties," she says. "We stood

✝ ✝ ✝

Like Wendy, Lori and I were strongly influenced by the image on a magazine cover. The photo on Time *magazine showed a mom holding a briefcase and a baby. The headline read, "The Case for Stay-at-Home Moms." We had already made our decision, but that magazine cover told us we were making the right choice at the right time. Other mothers were seeking ways to generate income for the family while fully committing themselves to their families, and some of those moms would become part of our team.*

✝ ✝ ✝

up for things—for women's rights, for equal treatment for African Americans, against the Vietnam war. I was, and am, on fire for making a difference."

Wendy started a Juice Plus virtual franchise because it made sense. Ethically and morally she had to share what she was learning about the relationship between nutrition and disease. Quickly, by accident, and without design, she became one of the top producers in the company. But her and her family's life of abundance truly arose from a deeper need to wake to passion and purpose every day, to die having made a bigger difference in the world and ultimately, for her and her husband to be able to design their lives filled with opportunity and choices.

The best part, she will tell you, is that she now knows God. Now, she believes that "He gave me every person, every word, and every piece of wisdom, and absolutely I give Him the glory for all of the blessings of our lives!"

A LIFE WITHOUT WORRY

Living an abundant life means you no longer have to worry. Worry is like a ball and chain. A multibillion-dollar medical community has grown up in recent decades because worry has become so epidemic. Sometimes it seems like they're inventing new problems so they can sell us the solution. There's a pill to fix this!

Politicians on both sides tell us what to worry about—or what to fear.

✝ ✝ ✝

Jesus said, "Do not worry."

Don't worry about your food.

Don't worry about your clothes.

Don't worry about your body.

Don't worry about tomorrow.

Your heavenly Father knows you need these

things, and He's on the case.

So stop worrying.

✝ ✝ ✝

People who worry a lot often want you to worry with them. Sometimes they have a true crisis, and your concern is warranted, and other times it's drama.

You might think I'm not a realist, or worse, that I don't care. But caring and worrying are two very different attitudes. Worry is rooted in fear, and it projects fear. Worry and fear anticipate the worst.

Caring is rooted in assurance, and it projects hope. Care. Don't worry.

Do not be afraid.

"Yea, though I walk through the valley of the shadow of death, I will fear no evil: for thou art with me." Those may be the most comforting words in the Bible. God is with me wherever I go. Why worry?

No problem is bigger than my God. He is bigger than any problem that I'm facing, and He tells me not to worry about it. So if He's bigger than my problem, and He says not to worry about it, then it's probably not going to help a lot if I do worry.

PAY THE PRICE

A life of abundance does not come simply because you've decided. There is a price to pay.

You want to be a concert pianist? At some point in time, every pianist you see on stage paid the price.

Once you've reached some success, many people see you the way you see that pianist. You make it look easy, and they want to be where you are. You have to show that person that the life you're living today didn't just happen. You started from nothing and paid the price. Somebody gave you a ladder down in the ditch you were in, but you still had to climb the ladder. It wasn't an escalator. You had to get from the valley to the mountaintop, and most people don't make it all the way up. They say they understand it, they see it, but when it comes time for the hard work, they don't get it done.

A lot of people want to play the piano. They take a lesson each week and learn to play, but the concert pianist took lessons and practiced every day for hours. A lot of people take piano lessons for ten years, but not a lot of people take piano lessons and practice enough to become an accomplished pianist. That's a big difference.

Anybody can make a life instead of making a living, but most people won't get out of their comfort zone and pay the price, so they just fall back to the minimum.

In our business, success requires paying the price for a season. It's a little like starting a motorboat. When you first push the throttle, the engine digs into the water and the bow rises up. The engine is working hard to get the boat moving forward. After a few seconds though, the bow levels out, and the boat is riding on top of the water instead of down in the water. It's called "planing out." When the boat is on plane, it responds easily to any adjustments you make, and at the helm you feel totally in control. You still have the throttle down, but the boat isn't working nearly as hard as before, and you feel like you're flying across the water.

You're living a life of abundance.

FIVE

Relationships

THE DAY I STARTED my business, I prayed that God would bring the right people across my path. I believe God creates every relationship, and whenever He brings a new person into my path, I'm wondering how can we do life together and do it better.

My kids say I'll talk to a brick wall. We'll step out of the elevator, and they ask, "Why did you have to talk to every person standing next to us?"

I answer, "Why not?"

If every person we come in contact with was placed there by God, then I want to know what He has in mind. Why did He bring us together? In the last three months I've sat next to six people on airplanes who all are now either customers or in the business with me. Here's one example.

Lori and I were in Canada for a Juice Plus event, and we went snowmobiling one day. We met a couple and their son while we were out, but of course, there isn't a lot of conversation when you're all out on separate snowmobiles. Near the end of the day, the man, John, asked in a British accent if we would take a photo of him with his wife and son. John, in his snow gear, had an unruly beard and three big loop earrings in one ear. He looked to be about my age, and his son looked about the same age as our son, Trey. We all climbed onto the shuttle bus and I sat beside John.

I asked if this was his first time in Canada and if he had been to the States. He and his wife were in Canada for ten days, and their son had been there for three months training to be a ski instructor. The boy was a senior in high school about to graduate, and in his gap year he wanted to teach skiing somewhere in Europe, or maybe Japan.

I told him that my son was a high school senior too, and for most of the ride we talked about our children. I mentioned my book *I Call Shotgun*, which is written as a series of letters from me and my co-author, Tommy Newberry, to our sons.

When we finally got around to occupation, John said he was a medic, which I assumed meant something like a paramedic in the U.S. But as we talked further, I realized he was a medical doctor, and he directed a drug and alcohol rehabilitation center.

We discussed the pros and cons of the national

✝ ✝ ✝

Are the valuable

relationships

in your life

benefiting

from the hours

you are investing

in them?

✝ ✝ ✝

health system. "I'm going on my own now," he said. "I'm kind of a hired gun, going to be an independent contractor, still paid by the national health system but I've got my own business. They're going to contract me."

After twenty minutes or longer, the conversation turned to my business, and I explained Juice Plus. He asked a lot of questions about the research behind the product, and then he said, "Can you get me some of this?"

Healthy relationships are not built around selling your product. Relationships are about seeing where your lives connect. People will continue to buy your product because it's good, but they'll try it for the first time because they like you, they trust you, and they respect you.

You make an investment in listening to someone's story, and they'll be willing to hear yours. The good thing is you can choose who you want to work with, so you're hearing their story not as bait so they'll listen to your story. You're hearing their story to see if they are somebody that God wants you to partner with. Sometimes you have to share stories before you have that wisdom. Where do you come together? Is it for ministry? Is it for your kids? Is it for your family? Is it in your business? Are they offering wisdom to be a better husband? A better parent?

For example, I met an electrician ten years ago, and he became my friend. When I have an emergency, I'm not going to the Yellow Pages. I'm calling my friend. Lori and met a young couple at church but lost contact with them when we moved. Years later we bought a lake house and were looking for a landscaper. We were in McDonald's one day and ran into George, our friend from years ago and miles away. He was a landscape contractor. We instantly reconnected and realized we knew someone we could trust to do good work at a fair price without having to negotiate.

When God gives me a new relationship, I don't stop with, "Okay, I know this person." I don't file business cards away to be forgotten. I pursue why I know this person. What can we do better now because this person is in my life? What connection can we make? What influence can we have? What battle needs to be won out there that we can win together? Sometimes we start right away. Or it may be twenty years before we work together.

RELENTLESS PURSUER

If there is a hierarchy of relationships, then for me it is God first, then my family, then my friends and business relationships.

In each of those relationships, the first step is knowing each other's names. God wants you to know your identity. If He were to call you something, give you a name, how would that name describe you to Him? Jesus gave Simon the name Peter, the rock. Jacob was given the name Israel, "he who wrestles with God." How does God know you? How are you unique?

I believe my identity in God is related to the way I am wired, as well as my favorite Bible verse:

As the deer pants for streams of water,

so my soul pants for you, my God.

– Psalm 42:1

I believe God sees me as a relentless pursuer. I always have been. When I was ten years old and taking my first tennis lesson with an old wooden racket, I wanted to start with a bang. I tried to serve the ball so hard, the racket slipped out of my hand, hit the rubber indoor court, and the butt of the racket came back up and cracked my jaw.

Because my earthly father was absent during my teenage years, I became a relentless pursuer of my

Holy Father to fill that void. My personal mission statement is, "To know God better every day through His Word, through prayer, and through the people He puts in my life. To be able to take that knowledge of Him and equip those that He brings across my path and do not know Him to know Him better." It's for me to pursue God in order to know Him, and then He has called me to share that knowledge of Him with others. Discovering my purpose was not an event but a process still going on today. I did learn and write a purpose statement, but it is ever evolving and being modified as life brings new environments, people, and changes.

Of all the earthly relationships God has given me to pursue, the greatest has been Lori Simril. We met through college ministry, and she was beautiful. She had an inner beauty that attracted me even more. I started falling for her the first time I saw her. On our first date I drove for an hour through rainy, rush-hour traffic to pick her up at her parents' house, then bring her back to a basketball game at Tech. Her dad had joked with her that that would be our first and last date, given her geographic undesirability, but he was way wrong. By the following Thanksgiving Lori and I were engaged.

The Simrils were a strong nuclear family—the

kind I hoped for our children. Her dad reminded me of my grandfather—practical and conservative, with all the common sense in the world. That stability was one of the foundations for us to build a family. It also was a foundation for building our business. Some of the most successful people I see in our company are husband/wife teams.

I didn't expect Lori and I would be working together when we married, but a year later she was pouring herself into the business—teeth, hair, and eyeballs—and I was right there with her. Her parents and my mom joined us, and then my Uncle David. Ours was the definition of a family business. When our first son, Trey, was born, the business was operating at a level that allowed Lori all the time she wanted with him.

CHANGING ROLES
IN THE RELATIONSHIP

Sometimes being a cheerleader hasn't worked.

When Lori and I married, we looked planned to have our first child after about three years, then two years later we would have our second. God gave us Trey right on (our) schedule, but then the plan stopped working. We had a miscarriage, and then another. Then a third. Over a seven-year period, we had four miscarriages and tubal pregnancies. Lori and I saw doctors, were tested, and did everything the doctors said to do.

I assumed my role as cheerleader, trying really hard to feel her pain. "We have Trey. He's an awesome son. Lot's of couples don't get to have a child. What if God only wants us to have Trey? What if that's God's plan for us? We can enjoy a great future with one child."

Lori didn't want me to be a cheerleader. She needed me to understand. She needed for her husband to show that he cared. Because, even though I believe life begins at conception, I was seeing these miscarriages as failed pregnancies. Lori felt each of them as a lost child who had lived inside her body for three months.

The more I tried to be positive, the more Lori became sad.

I couldn't figure it out by myself, and I didn't seem to be getting the right answers through my prayers. I shared my problems with three friends I had grown close to through church, then a men's retreat in North Carolina. Ken, George, Rick, and I met for breakfast almost every week, almost never with an agenda. We were just there for each other. I asked them, "What do I say when she's so sad and so upset and so frustrated and so mad at God and all these things?"

"You just need to be there," they said. "There's nothing you can say to fix it or to make the hurt go away. Just be there in that moment with her."

So that's what I tried to do. Then in the middle of my trying to be sensitive at home, Lori's doctor would give her new hope, only to have that bubble burst weeks later. I finally had to speak to the doctor in the hall and tell her, "Unless you want to live at our house and see Lori's hope snatched away from her month after month, you'd better stop giving her false hope."

Then a book arrived in the mail, Dr. James Dobson's *When God Doesn't Make Sense*. Dr. Dobson didn't attempt to explain what he called the "awesome why"—why we experience pain and why bad things happen to good people. He simply reminded us in a powerful way, with illustrations of other hurting people, "that neither death nor life, neither angels nor demons, neither the present nor the future, nor any powers, neither height nor depth, nor anything else in all creation, will be able to separate us from the love of God that is in Christ Jesus our Lord" (Romans 8:38-39).

In time Lori became pregnant again, and she delivered a healthy baby girl. In our joy we remembered Proverbs 13:12, "Hope deferred makes the heart sick, but a longing fulfilled is a tree of life." So we named our daughter Hope; our hope deferred had become our longing fulfilled. Then Zach was born, with the zeal of his father, and our family was complete.

PERSONS OF PEACE

Nothing we own in this world is more important than our relationships with other people. Corporations use the term *relational capital* to place a value on their relationships with customers and vendors. When I use the words *relational capital,* they remind me how important other people are to my business and my life.

I grew up in the Baptist church, and all my life I have been taught evangelism and discipleship. Every Sunday, and at every conference I went to as a teenager, I was taught how to share the Gospel and how to train others to share. I've been through every Baptist Sunday school lesson on evangelism, learned about the Good News Glove and how to share the Gospel using tracts, brochures, or the Four Spiritual Laws. In addition to teaching me how to share my faith, those years of training gave me confidence that I could succeed in a business that relies on relationships.

I learned that when Jesus was ready to leave this

world, He told His disciples they could do even more than He did if they relied on persons of peace. He defined a person of peace as someone who would make available whatever they had—shelter, food, safety, relationships—in a place where His mission was moving into new territory.

Jesus said His message had to be taken into other cities and other countries. It had to spread. Here's how He told them to spread it: When you go into a town and you go into a home, if the people living there accept your message and welcome you, they will feed you. They will use their resources in that town to equip you and help you stay longer and grow. If not, then move on until you find one who will.

I learned about the Apostle Paul, the greatest Christian evangelist ever, and his impact on the early church. Paul also relied on persons of peace. He would meet someone who took on the responsibility of spreading the message, then Paul would go to his next stop, leaving his new leader behind to carry on his work. Paul knew that sometimes the person he had left behind needed to be encouraged, and he would either send someone, write a letter, or go back a second time.

I learned early on that the business model for biblical evangelism works in our businesses. Persons of peace open up a new territory or open up new areas of influence that we don't have. Conversely, in our business, if you have a friend you really want to work with, but they don't open up their resources to you, that's okay. They're still your friend, but you've got to move on with your business.

Many of my closest friends are not in business with me. But we still support each other, and they have recommended others who now work with me.

You're Either Buying or Selling

A friend once told me, "Every time you interact with somebody, in every conversation, somebody is buying and somebody is selling."

You may be telling your friend about a movie or a book or a pair of shoes, and if you really believe in what you're talking about, you're selling. You're trying to convince your friend that the movie you watched or the book you read is worth watching or reading. This is the definition of word-of-mouth marketing; you're "selling" a product or service that you've become passionate about.

If, on the other hand, you're not totally committed and your friend disagrees with your opinion, then the conversation might turn completely around and transform you into a buyer of his opinion.

Now imagine you're talking about a product you're selling. If you really understand the product, believe in the product, and are absolutely convinced the product is bulletproof, then you will confidently remain in sales mode versus buy mode. Because even if the other person rejects what you're offering, or tries to sell you something else, you're going to believe in your product.

But if your belief is weak and you're not committed to what you're doing, then you go into a situation trying to sell something awesome—your passion, your purpose, your dream, your vision, your product—the other person may have a stronger opposing belief, and you could end up being the buyer.

LEARNING FROM THE SOWER

The most discouraging time for people who are new to sales can be those early days, when their results don't align with their expectations. They've made a list of their friends, family, and acquaintances, and they've started making calls, anticipating ten sales in the first eleven calls.

Do you really think you're that good? Or do you enjoy having high-pressure conversations with your friends?

Several years ago Bruce Wilkinson, founder of

✝ ✝ ✝

God owns it all.

The seeds you sow.

The soil you grow in.

The relationships you make.

God owns it all, and God is in charge,

whether you acknowledge that or not.

You can live your life acknowledging

He is charge and get on His agenda

for your life. Or you can decide

to live your own life,

but He is still in charge.

✝ ✝ ✝

Walk Thru the Bible Ministries and author of *The Prayer of Jabez*, spoke at our prayer breakfast before the Juice Plus national conference. He compared sales with the Parable of the Sower.

"The sower went out to sow; and as he sowed, some seeds fell beside the road, and the birds came and ate them up. Others fell on the rocky places, where they did not have much soil; and immediately they sprang up, because they had no depth of soil. But when the sun had risen, they were scorched; and because they had no root, they withered away. Others fell among the thorns, and the thorns came up and choked them out. And others fell on the good soil and yielded a crop, some a hundredfold, some sixty, and some thirty."

Bruce explained that in connecting with others, you are sowing seeds, and you have no control over the outcome. If you're talking with them about a business opportunity, you can plant seeds with a great product, a great company, and a powerful mission. You may know this person—and absolutely know the business is right for them. You have a great time together, and feel the energy going both directions.

Then they don't do it, and you know in your heart that they're making a huge mistake. So you try to push that person. *I've got to make them do it*, you think.

And when they don't, you feel like you've failed.

But sometimes these decisions have nothing to do with you. They're about the soil the seed falls on. Turning to the parable, Bruce explained that we're not called to change the soil. We keep sowing seed.

Some of that seed will end up scorched on the roadside, and some will find shallow soil among the rocks and take root but never thrive. Wait. Something in their life has so distracted them, you can't get their attention.

Others may be choked by weeds—turmoil, crisis, or tragedy in their lives—and they need a shoulder to lean on. Your role may not be to lead them into a new business but to listen and provide that shoulder. God may have put you at that intersection for a different purpose.

Then a seed falls on good soil; the person you're connecting with is listening and ready to respond to your offer.

If you keep sowing seeds, you will realize in the best-case scenario, 25 percent of the people you connect with will do something right now. That doesn't mean you've wasted 75 percent of your seeds. You've sowed seed into a lot of the right people, who are simply not ready. And many will never be in the right soil to respond to your message. You have to wait till they're in different soil when they're ready to do something.

What appears to you a lack of success is the truth in the Parable of the Sower. You don't need a new sales pitch or a new script. You're not doing anything wrong. You're just not sowing enough seeds.

Keep in touch with the ones who are not growing. You may not be able to change the soil, but you can be available when they're ready.

Then turn your attention to the ones in the good soil and develop them. They're ready.

If your goal is ten customers in your business, don't think you'll get there by talking to eleven people. In your disappointment, you'll damage important relationships. Instead, engage forty or fifty people in wonderful life-change conversations, knowing that when they're ready, you'll be ready.

IRON SHARPENS IRON

I had never heard of an accountability group until I became part of one. We actually didn't call ourselves accountability partners. We were just friends who met in a Bible study, went to a men's retreat together, and started getting together for breakfast at least once a week, trying to figure out how to do life. Some weeks, when living was especially complicated, we met three or four times. Ken, George, Rick, and me. George would say that Rick and I were more fundamental in our beliefs. I might have labeled George "liberal." Ken, who was our Bible study leader and the originator of the smaller group, was the steady influence.

Over the last twenty-five years we've supported each other through job changes, job losses, and serious financial difficulty; infertility crises; the challenges of children and of death—deep, deep stuff.

We've celebrated childbirths and adoptions, financial success, and the obvious moving of God in our lives. God used our friendship to literally save George's life.

As iron sharpens iron, so one person

sharpens another.

— Proverbs 27:17

For some time George said he had felt like the "odd man out" in our group—as if our more conservative interpretation of biblical truth indicated judgment. Or that three of us as entrepreneurs thought less of him because he had a corporate job. We were in our midthirties when he was struggling with his job and his marriage, and his father was in a nursing home in Louisiana. The pressure kept building for him, and he was frustrated that he wasn't connecting with the three of us the way he wanted. One day he literally said, "To hell with it," resigned from his job, and went to work for a company in Louisiana. Over the next two years George would go through three major job changes, move from Atlanta to Louisiana to Dallas and back to Atlanta.

Here's how close our group was: Ken and his wife sold their house before their new house was finished, and they needed a place to live for several months. George and his wife had extra room, so they invited the Morrows to live with them.

Three months later, on George's fortieth birthday, the company he was working for was sold. The new owners immediately began layoffs, including George. For the first time in his life, he was unemployed. He was broken. Looking back on those dark days, George says the Lord put the Morrows in his house to keep him from hitting absolute rock bottom. "I was at my limit in what I could do and communicate," he says.

Ken prayed with him, encouraged him, then connected him with his own son, Jason, who owned a small computer business. George worked with Jason in sales for several months, but in August Jason had to tell him, "George, we can't afford to pay you any more. We're happy to pay you a commission on what you bring in, but that's all we can do."

Driving home that night, unemployed for the second time in his life, George pulled the car to the side of the road and wept. Then he cried out to God, "Lord, I can't do this anymore. I can't." That morning he had stuck a devotional book by Anne Graham Lotz in his briefcase, even though he almost never read it. Sitting in the car he reached for the book and opened it to September 4. At the top of the page were the words of Jesus, "What I'm doing right now you don't understand, but you will know after this."

The statement was for George, and when he read it, he felt a peace sweeping over him like he had never experienced.

Over the next several months, opportunities opened up for George leading him to Mississippi where he is now in partnership with a multimillion-dollar (sales) company selling water and wastewater treatment equipment. He has also connected with a small group of men he meets with weekly who are "figuring out what it looks like to love God with all our heart, soul, mind, and strength." George is the youngest in the group; the oldest is in his mideighties.

In prayer, in Scripture, and seeking God's truth alongside other men, George says he now knows, "Society says bust your butt—the harder you work, the better off you'll be. Nothing could be further from the truth. I'm working hard, but I'm not providing. The Lord is providing. God is asking, 'Do you really trust Me?' That's a huge revelation.

"I had to go through a process and get to the place where I could hear God speak. He was speaking all along, but I didn't listen."

George uses his company and its work in waste-water treatment as an analogy for his life. "A lot of unpleasant things go down a sewer. God had to humble me."

The unpleasantness was not all financial. There came a time when George was at a difficult point in his marriage. Ken and I encouraged him (implored him) not to give up. We believed God could rebuild what he and Tammie were losing. George says now, "What God has done to restore us is so much greater than I could ask for"—even given them an adopted child when they had nearly given up on the possibility.

We all deal with life and its challenges so differently

and make assumptions about what another person thinks. Meeting with the same three guys week after week, year after year, allowed us to be completely transparent with each other.

We walked with Rick as he dealt with the brain cancer that took his life before his forty-fifth birthday. We were with George through his trials. And they all supported and encouraged me when Lori and I spent our years in the desert of infertility.

With George in Mississippi, only Ken and I continue to meet regularly, but the three of us remain close, talking often, attempting to sharpen one another, and praying for each other daily.

INVESTING RELATIONAL CAPITAL

Relational capital has to be treated like any other asset we're called to be stewards over. Our society does a good job of putting time and money front and center. For decades companies competed to develop the most effective paper calendar, from *Franklin Day Planners* to *365 Days of Garfield*. Beginning with the Palm Pilot and then the Blackberry, they've now finally developed an electronic calendar for smartphones that helps us manage our time. Entire cable channels, newspapers, and magazines are dedicated to the management and

✝ ✝ ✝

Whatever God puts before me I'll go after energetically—especially the relationships He brings. Nothing is greater than connecting with the right person at the right time, because together we can accomplish more than we could have alone.

✝ ✝ ✝

stewardship of our financial resources.

The most overlooked asset, and the one that delivers the greatest reward, is relationships. Like any other capital, relational capital cannot be ignored. You can withdraw from a relationship so much and not be investing back into it.

The American mind-set today is: build your business, build your business, build your business. Too many people build their businesses at the expense of relationships. The greatest companies, on the other hand, first build relationships with integrity, and then the business grows. Chick-fil-A, based in Atlanta, is rated America's favorite fast-food restaurant. It is the only restaurant company listed among the best companies to work for by the *Wall Street Journal*. And sales per restaurant are higher at Chick-fil-A than any other chain. So how did they get to be so good? By focusing first on relationships with customers and employees. I experience the payoff of their investment every time I'm greeted by a pleasant person behind the counter. They look me in the eye and engage me personally. In those few seconds together, we have a relationship. And when I thank them for their service, they always reply, "My pleasure." No wonder they're at the top in every measurement, including customer loyalty.

WHEN WORK IS A PLEASURE

Like my classmates at Georgia Tech, I ran the interview gauntlet when I graduated from college. The corporate opportunities at IBM, Proctor & Gamble, and others looked interesting, but my home was Atlanta, and I didn't want to move to Bowling Green, Kentucky, or Green Bay, Wisconsin. Not even for a good salary and a company car. Still, with my business degree, I assumed a corporate career of some sort was my future. My mom had succeeded in direct sales, but that was her world, not mine. Or so I thought.

God prepares us for seasons of life and we never even realize it until we're there. My teenage years driving a truck and slugging aloe vera jugs around left me thinking, "She's just in there talking and I'm sweating, carrying gallon jugs around." I thought my manual labor was the hard job.

Then I learned that the hard job is the one you are not called to. When you respond to your calling, your job doesn't feel like work.

Even though I understood how direct sales companies worked, I was skeptical the night Lori and I met Fran and her husband to discuss their opportunity. As it turned out, the opportunity they presented was right in my wheelhouse. I'm called to be in relationship with other people, and that's the opportunity she was offering.

After the industrial revolution and the technology revolution, the human side of business is winning again. We have a growing economy based on community and trust. Technology puts us in instant contact with people across the globe, so I can visit with my associates in Europe as easily and personally as my next-door neighbors.

From a Corporate Mind-set to a People Mind-set

One of the most powerful God moments in my life occurred standing under a goalpost in Texas Stadium, home of the Dallas Cowboys, at a Promise Keepers event with Mick Daly. Surrounded by thousands of other men on the field and up in the stands, Mick and I decided together to be the men, husbands, fathers, and grandfathers that God called us to be. By that time Mick and I had already been working together for several years.

Before we met, Mick had walked away from a twenty-three-year career in management with IBM to begin a whole new career that would allow his family to stay in the United States. His wife, Jenny, wondered if he had lost his mind.

Jenny and Mick were citizens of the United Kingdom, but at the end of a three-year stint with IBM in Dallas, Texas, the Dalys asked the company for a permanent position in the United States. IBM said no, they would have to return to the UK. Jenny assumed that was the end of it; they were going home.

"Our boys were in high school, and they wanted to stay," she recalls. "Their lives centered around sports and their friends in Dallas. But after twenty-three years with IBM, Mick didn't know anything else, and we didn't have any other options."

Mick thought otherwise.

"I believed our lives would be better if we stayed in the United States, even if that meant leaving the company," Mick says. "I couldn't be precise about what that would look like, but it was a decision for freedom."

IBM allowed Mick to work as an independent contractor in Dallas for one year while he sought business opportunities and worked with an attorney to attain the right legal status to stay.

"We didn't immediately experience the freedom we sought," he says. "The price of leaving the corporation was a loss of security. I had, and still have, a sense of guilt that I pulled the rug of security out from under Jenny in my ignorance and selfishness, not understanding how important financial security is to her."

"Mick is a pioneer," Jenny explains. "I'm a settler. However, when we discussed whether to go back or stay, we both agreed our marriage was the most important thing, even if we failed financially."

As it turned out, the opportunity they were looking for came from one of our Juice Plus team who was also working with IBM. "My boss lived in Raleigh, North Carolina," Mick recalls, "and he introduced us to this company. He flew in to Dallas for my final IBM departmental meeting, and afterward he came to my office and closed the door. He gave me a VHS tape about the virtual franchise. I watched it and believed that was the answer."

Mick joined the company and had one year to build a network strong enough to support his family before his consulting contract with IBM would expire.

"As it turned out," he says, "that first year I was very unsuccessful. I was an arrogant, corporate management-trained fool trying to reinvent the wheel because I thought I could do it better."

Jenny interrupts and says, "Mick exaggerates. But he was unteachable."

The Dalys survived on their savings, which carried them into their second year. Mick needed to become a National Marketing Director for both the benefits and the income ("Honestly, for the recognition too!").

"We had no Plan B," he says. "When you have an escape route, a Plan B or C or D, it's easy to get distracted and stop what you're doing. I couldn't afford to get distracted. I was fully committed.

"My first three years with the company were humbling for me, and yet that experience may have been the greatest benefit. In those three years I learned more about people and how they are motivated than I had in twenty-three years of corporate management and training. I understood the difference between management and leadership. Those lessons carried into other areas of our lives."

✝ ✝ ✝

Our greatest needs

are met by building

into other people's lives.

— Mick Daly

✝ ✝ ✝

One lesson Mick learned was that he needed Jenny to be his business partner, not his secretary. "I had a secretary all those years at IBM, and I didn't give it a second thought. That would be Jenny's role. Then after a year or two she sat me down and said, 'We need to talk. . . .'"

"Over time working together in the business, we recognized each other's talents," Jenny says. "Mick sees the big picture. He's a leader. He's great on the computer. I love customer care and personal interactions. I'm a former schoolteacher, and I like to teach people how to take control of their health and how to build a home-based business."

As I mentioned earlier, many of the top people in our business are couples who have learned to work together, just like Lori and I started out as newlyweds singing from the same hymnal to build a business and fill a financial void in our lives.

"Now when we talk with young couples," Jenny says, "we explain how the business helped us learn and celebrate our differences, and how our different strengths build our marriage and our business." This year they will celebrate forty-five years of marriage.

After their boys left for college, Mick and Jenny sold their house in Dallas and followed another dream, traveling around the country for four years in an RV. Now they've settled in Eagle, Colorado. "Our boys and their families live five minutes away from us here," Mick says. "God has given us so much more than we deserve. We never even dreamed of the life we have ended up living, and we're in awe of everything that has transpired for us."

SIX

MODERN-DAY TENT MAKING

I KNOW SO MANY PEOPLE who have heart and passion for ministry, but they're terrible at fundraising. They spend 70 percent of their time raising money because it's not their strength, leaving only 30 percent for the ministry. It's a broken fundraising model for ministry.

I believe a better model is modern-day tent making.

The Apostle Paul in the New Testament was the church's greatest evangelist ever, traveling the known world to spread the Gospel, yet he never quit his job as a tent maker. By generating revenue from his work, Paul was able to financially support his ministry without depending on those he was serving. He made tents in Galatia, Corinth, Thessalonica, and Ephesus, and perhaps other places as well.

But Paul's tent making wasn't just about money. His job took him to places and put him side by side with people who would never have met him in the synagogue. Often our life purpose is not the same as our vocation, but our vocation can provide the financial wherewithal to engage our purpose.

Your vocation can be your path for doing God's business. How many people will you be in front of in your work that you would never see if you were in an office at church all day?

REST, THEN WORK

My wife and children will tell you that on most days, I do very little work in the evening. But I've done a whole lot before four o'clock.

God rested, and then on the first day He created. That is the way of creation. Rest, then create. What the world does is work so hard until they collapse. God says rest so you can work well. Your rest has to come first. My kids think I'm nuts because they want to stay up and do things late at night. I tell them, "It's time for me to go bed, dude, and I'm going to bed."

I need to get up early. Since I was a teenager and learned about quiet time in the morning, I've made that my pattern: start the day, put God first in quiet time, then plan the rest of the day undistracted. Before we had children, I could do that at six o'clock. When Lori and I had children, I got up at four so I could

MAKE A LIFE, NOT JUST A LIVING

have my quiet time and then family time in the morning. My oldest son is twenty-five, and for twenty-five years, I've been up early almost every morning.

Someone asked me what I do in that time, and I said, "In all honesty, I just create two hours of quiet, and it kind of unfolds with God every day." There is no regimen.

Sometimes I read my Bible. I may read a great book. Or focus on the day, seeking God's wisdom on how to take it on effectively—acknowledging that it's His day, not mine.

Sometimes I don't even get my Bible out. It's just God helping me see through His lens what's going on in my life. Being still and quiet and not letting all the buzzes and beeps and whistles and bells and noises that the world throws at me get in the way.

I get my sleep and I get up early and I seize the day. Then in the afternoon I'm running or playing tennis, and enjoying relationships with my family and friends.

LEAVE ROOM IN THE MARGINS FOR HEALTHY RELATIONSHIPS

Notice the space between the type and the edge of this page. Whether you're holding an actual book or an e-reader, that margin of blank space surrounding

147

the type adds up to more than one-third of the page. What a waste! We could fill that space with text and save a third of the paper.

Imagine, though, how the page would look with type running from edge to edge, top to bottom.

Our eyes and our brains need to rest, and the margins give them the break they need.

Another of my favorite books is *Margin*, by Dr. Richard Swenson. Dr. Swenson uses the analogy of a printed page to represent our lives. A type-A person who has tons of people in their life can allow the calendar to fill up quickly with people interactions. Each of those interactions is enjoyable, fulfilling, and sometimes financially rewarding. Meetings with coworkers, an appointment with the pastor, coffee with a friend, parent-teacher conference, lunch with an accountability partner, soccer game, ballet recital, and on it goes until your life has no white space left at the edges.

It took me a long time to learn to say no, and I still struggle. It's easy to say no to the bad ideas, but if you don't say no to some good things, then you won't do anything well. Saying no leaves space at the margins for rejuvenation. If you're going to build relationships, leave room in the margins. Be available for unexpected opportunities.

✝ ✝ ✝

We prepare for rainy day or an adventure.

We provide for our loved ones. Money

should never be the primary goal, but rather

the byproduct of what fuels a higher call-

ing. When you're entrusted with financial

capital, you must invest it wisely. Most of

us never have enough available to think

we can start our own business. That's the

beauty of the virtual franchise. It only takes

$50 to start. People who don't have money

can build something big by relying on their

relational capital.

✝ ✝ ✝

✝ ✝ ✝

The world teaches

you to manage.

God teaches

you to be a steward,

because He created it all,

including time.

✝ ✝ ✝

I love to see a Bible whose owner has written notes in the margins—using those white spaces for questions, to explore ideas, or to make notes on how God spoke through a particular verse on a particular day. When my pastor, Buddy Hoffman, is asked to conduct a funeral, he asks for the person's Bible for a few days so he can see what's been written in the margins. Those words say much about the person.

Time: The Truest Measure

Time is the truest outward measurement of why one person is successful and another is not. It's the only resource we all have the same amount of. Bill Gates, Warren Buffett, you, and I all have twenty-four hours every day. No more. No less. As long as you are in pursuit of that twenty-fifth hour, you're going to fail. Successful people set boundaries. They maintain balance.

Succeed by Delegating

Our business (and our nation) celebrates the success of individuals—the self-made success, the woman who pulled herself up by her bootstraps.

I join the applause of the successful individual, but I see even greater success in people who willingly share responsibilities and rewards. When I hired an assistant to help me with certain clerical responsibilities, I was concerned about the short-term impact on our cash flow. It turned out to be immediate and positive. Suddenly I could delegate time-consuming tasks and free myself for the work I love most and do best.

START WELL, FINISH WELL

I do my best work when the important aligns with the urgent.

If you're going to start something, make sure you see it through to the end. Finish it well. Don't just start well; finish well too.

You might think as you approach the finish line, *Looks like I'm running out of time.*

Instead, you should be thinking, *Oh my gosh, I'm almost out of time. I need to pull in all my resources, because I said I was going to do this, and I'm going to get it done.*

Our youngest son, Zach, graduated from high school while I was writing this book. At his school, students are exempt from final exams as long as they have an A in the class. Zach was going into the final week of school with a 90 in one class and one more big test—so big that it could have pulled him back to a B if he didn't do well. All of a sudden I saw Zach rallying. The urgent aligned with the important.

It's our nature to procrastinate—put off doing the things we don't want to do, even when they're important. Then we face a deadline, like Zach's test and the opportunity to exempt a final exam, and the important becomes urgent. He brought the zeal and energy required to prepare for the test and exempt his exam.

You may have seen this diagram:

URGENT	URGENT
NOT IMPORTANT	IMPORTANT
NOT URGENT	NOT URGENT
NOT IMPORTANT	IMPORTANT

You want to dwell in the top right URGENT/ IMPORTANT quadrant.

Too many times we allow the unimportant to become urgent because we allow urgency to run our lives. When we effectively filter out the unimportant, often by delegating it to someone else, then we can expend our energy on the things that are most important to us.

Another thing that happens is people dump

their urgent on you. You have to put it through your filter and ask, "Is that important? Is that a me thing?" Otherwise you might end up feeding somebody else's monkey. That's a concept I read about years ago, and it changed my life: don't feed somebody else's monkey.

The "monkey" is the monkey on your back. Everybody has monkeys, also known as responsibilities.

In 1974 the *Harvard Business Review* published an essay titled "Who's Got the Monkey?" The article was reprinted in 1999 with a commentary by Stephen R. Covey and has been one of *HBR*'s two best-selling reprints ever. The monkey is a big, big deal.

If you feed someone else's monkey, they're going to let you feed it, and that will diminish your ability to fulfill your own responsibilities. So you have to decide you're going to feed the monkeys you want to feed. There are a lot of hungry monkeys, and you're not called to feed all of them even if you could.

Most of the time no one is going to let their monkeys starve. It's not the world's fault for pushing monkeys at you. You've got to filter them.

STEWARDSHIP OF ADVENTURE

"It's amazing what you can live without," Michelle Barnett says. She and her husband, Brian, live and

✢ ✢ ✢

Stewardship is a responsibility, not a require-

ment. We are responsible for what we have,

whether it is a little or a lot.

✢ ✢ ✢

travel in a motor home—250 square feet. They left their home in Texas planning to cover the entire United States while avoiding winter anywhere along the way. (It's no fun to drive an RV in the snow.)

Michelle and Brian are an ultimate seize-the-day couple. They met in Austin, Texas, and fell in love. Then Brian left for an eleven-month, eleven-country mission trip. When he returned, they married and started designing a life they wanted together. Brian has an MBA, so he considered seeking a corporate position. But Michelle had a Juice Plus virtual franchise, and they decided to seek the freedom that working together in this venture would allow. Their Juice Plus success has also allowed Michelle to pursue her dream of building Nourish-Mint LLC, a nation-wide team of health coaches who are helping families and individuals make healthy living choices through nutrition counseling and Juice Plus.

Once their journey was conceived, they stored their furniture, bought an RV, and hit the road, running their businesses from across the country with cell phones and laptops. They work with people from Hawaii to Rhode Island, meal planning, creating bio-individual health plans, and offering nutrition education. They help people make one simple change by eliminating different food groups to identify allergies and sensitivities that contribute to their health problems. They practice and teach whole food living through incorporating more beneficial foods, so that they and their clients are not just living, but thriving. Week by week they coach and take care of their clients and team by phone, text, and e-mail—from the road.

They drive awhile, then stay awhile when they find a national park or other site of interest to explore. This lifestyle satisfies both their adventurous hearts and their calling to make a difference. They're doing all this in the first half of their lives—not waiting to make their dreams a reality.

"The surprising thing on this trip for me," Michelle says, "is that I am a type-A planner, always with a schedule. This trip made me so much more flexible and spontaneous. Some weeks we have no cell service, and I have to cancel my scheduled calls, or something breaks on the RV and our plans change. I'm seeing myself learn to adapt and not stress, and learn to trust God more in the process."

✝ ✝ ✝

My friend and best-selling author Tommy

Newberry closes his e-mail with,

"Remember, your success blesses others."

Let the fruit of your success flow freely

through you to others around you.

✝ ✝ ✝

SEVEN
PASSING THE BATON

WE NEVER OUTGROW the need for mentors in our lives. My mentors led me to find God's purpose for my life, led me to be zealous in what I pursued, offered guidance as I built a business and raised a family. Then there came a time when I had soaked up so much, it seemed like a switch went off, though it wasn't that drastic. God just let me know that it was time to pour back into others. Hindsight allows you to package up some of the wisdom others have shared and give it to someone else. That's the challenge I face as my children move into their adult lives, Lori and I have become grandparents, and the leaders we recruited into the business grow as mentors themselves. We are passing the baton to the next generation.

You're familiar with the illustration. A great collegiate track coach builds a winning relay team by recruiting fast runners and teaching them how to pass the baton without breaking stride.

The concept works in families, churches, and businesses. You learn to run the race, but as long as you're running alone, you're limiting your impact. In business, you're literally trading hours for dollars. Then you learn to connect with the next person—to pass the baton without dropping it or breaking stride.

How long are two hands on the baton? You can't tell somebody what to do and expect them to do it right the first time. They want a piece of you. They want to understand how you do it. People believe and accept your message because you help them achieve their vision—you keep your hand on the baton just long enough for them to then run on their own.

Too many people short-circuit the handoff. They give a list of ten steps, or say, "Here's a video. Watch this, then go out and do it."

Everybody is different. Each passing of the baton is unique.

Sometimes we pass a baton without realizing it. "God rarely allows a person to see how great a blessing he is to others." That declaration by Oswald Chambers, in his book *My Utmost for His Highest*, reminds me that we are always making an impact on others—especially young people—whether we know it or not. Where our children are concerned, they are watching what we do much more closely than listening to what we say.

I wrote early in this book that my father was not around for my teenage years. Yet he still had an impact, especially when I was younger.

My brother and I would play hide-and-seek in his furniture store, and buy Cokes in a bottle for a dime from the machine in the back. We made a lot of memories there. Sometimes some of the Atlanta Falcons football players would come in while I was there, and I would watch awestruck as Dad visited with them. NFL players in those days made a lot less money than they do today, and Dad hired some of them to help collect debts. There was never anything rough or threatening, but I'm sure seeing a Falcons linebacker at your door reminding you that you owed money to Beavers Furniture improved Dad's collections.

Another of Dad's collectors, Stan, was a big guy but not a football player. One night Stan was shot. The incident was unrelated to the store, but Stan was Dad's friend, so he went to the hospital to be with him. When he got there, Stan was unconscious. He had lost a lot of blood and needed a transfusion to save his life. But as Jehovah's Witnesses, his family protested.

Dad was beside himself, and he argued to take the steps to save Stan's life. My childhood memories of that event lack details, except for how upset my father was that church "rules" might cost his friend's life. When I was older and learned about the potential negative impact of legalism, I remembered Dad caring for Stan, and the little piece of himself he passed along to me.

POWER TO FLOWING THROUGH US

I went on a mission trip to New York when I was a teenager and helped lead vacation Bible school for children there. The fatherless problem wasn't talked about as much then, but it was present in the kids we saw. And yet we saw true joy in so many of them. We were young and excited, and they knew somebody loved and cared about them. That connection—that place where our mission met their need—allowed the power of God to flow through us. He showed us how we could join Him in His work. We saw real fruit, and the experience was high-octane fuel for mission.

CHOOSING FIRST FRIENDS

As young parents, until our children knew how to choose friends wisely, Lori and I were involved in the process of choosing for them. The children they hung around were going to have a huge impact in their life, so we were not leaving that to chance.

✝ ✝ ✝

"Don't cry because it's over,

smile because it happened."

— Dr. Seuss

That's a powerful statement for a parent,

as your youngest child graduates from high

school. Some things deserve a tear, and Lori

and I have both shed some tears.

But if you're crying, cry in celebration

of the accomplishment, not in sadness

that it's over.

✝ ✝ ✝

AT THE EDGE OF ADULTHOOD

More recently our church has sponsored thirty international high school students on a three-month visit to the United States. They lived in homes with families and went to school at a local university.

They were beautiful kids, all of them. They spoke English well, greeted you with a big smile and a handshake, and were on the lookout for fun. And like teenagers anywhere, they were looking for what's next in life. They're at the edge of becoming adults in a country where unemployment is very high. They believe in God and creation, but they had not studied Scripture. We gave them their first Bibles.

Everybody is searching for meaningful life. In their country, capitalism and making a lot of money doesn't cross their mind. Life is about survival. My prayer for them is that they learn that God cares. God has a mission for them. He wired them to pursue a mission, a purpose. We encouraged them to seek that mission. They may already have missed a potential kairos moment, but when God sees you're willing and available, He'll come back. When the students realize God has a plan, He'll create another kairos moment, and they'll be ready.

I shared my story with them and encouraged them to share their stories when they returned home.

The only way people find out about your mission and join it is hearing you tell your story about your relationship with God.

INSPIRING HEALTHY LIVING

Juice Plus has committed to putting a Tower Garden in every Boys and Girls Club in America. We're giving away 10 million meals in the next five years. We hope to inspire healthy living—to show the next generation how delicious fresh food can be, and how much fun they can have growing it themselves.

The concept of healthy living can be a heavy baton for some to carry. They see so many simultaneous goals and just as many obstacles, they just give up.

So we encourage them not to change everything this week, but to make One Simple Change. Any of these simple changes can make a positive impact:

Drink more water.
Sleep more, stress less.
Eat more whole foods.
Get more exercise.

Any one of these simple changes can build success, become a habit, and create momentum toward a making a healthy life.

✝ ✝ ✝

I encourage everyone who works with us to

create their own brand. But the goal is for us

to be parallel and in sync with each other. So

in my message of "Make a Life," I can share

my story and my branding, but my goal is to

be able to give them the megaphone to tell

their own story of how they made a life.

✝ ✝ ✝

STEPHEN RITZ' PASSION FOR KIDS

Stephen Ritz was a middle-school special-education teacher in South Bronx, and the school gave him all of the emotionally handicapped kids. Basically, he says, the people wanted him to perpetuate the status quo and make sure these kids stayed inside the class and didn't hurt anybody else or themselves. There were no expectations for these kids. It was a classically failed system; these kids were in and out of the criminal justice system. They were kids that people wrote off, and society made a good living off making sure they stayed written off. Stephen was determined to change that, and as he got to know them better, he realized they were some of the nicest, most talented, most capacity-rich people he had ever met.

It was his duty, he believed, his obligation to move them from being "apart from" to being "a part of" in ways that motivated everybody. That was his motivation.

Stephen was not trained or prepared for the task. The Bronx, where he had grown up, was burnt to a crisp when he graduated from college. He had no idea what he was going to do for a living, so he took a test to become a teacher. There was a teaching crisis at the time, so when he passed the test and showed up on time for an interview, they hired him.

He had no passion for teaching, but he had a passion for people, so he took that passion to school, where the system was stacked against his kids. Looking back, Stephen says the fact that anyone let him in the room with a bunch of kids was "kind of hilarious. It was like one big episode of *The Little Rascals*," he recalls, "like the time we had a 22-foot snake in the classroom, and it got away. They had to close the school. Then one weekend before the city had Metro cards, we went into the subways for the weekend and raced around the city in a contest to see who could hit every single stop without coming out—just one token. The kids learned how to develop algorithms and about closed systems and systems planning. We also had the first group of kids who were special needs to compete in the Five Borough Bike Tour."

Years later Stephen was assigned seventeen kids, all of whom came out of jail. Statistically, we know kids who come out of jail between the ages of seventeen and twenty-one are back in jail within two years.

✢ ✢ ✢

"The single biggest prognosticator for a

child's success in life is having access to one

kind, caring adult. I am going

to be that kind, caring adult."

— Stephen Ritz

✢ ✢ ✢

Stephen was determined to keep that from happening by loving his kids until they learned to love themselves. That was his job, he says. He was determined to treat them the way he wanted his daughter treated. At that time, Stephen had a daughter in second grade, and she came to school with him, to that class, every day.

Those kids saw how he taught his daughter, and his daughter saw how he taught those kids. (Fast forward ten years later, she wrote a college essay, "My Family of Non-Biological Brothers, the Seventeen Kids in My Father's Class.")

Someone sent Stephen a box of onions that he tossed behind the radiator so the kids wouldn't find them and throw them in class. After a few weeks something in that direction caught his eye, and he turned to see bright yellow daffodil blooms. Those bulbs weren't onions at all! The heat from the radiator had forced the daffodils into bloom, and in that moment Stephen realized that living, growing, green plants were another opportunity to connect with his kids. He knew nothing about farming, and nothing about gardening. (To this day, he says he still doesn't. But his kids do.) Stephen had an idea.

He and the kids started landscaping abandoned lots to beautify their neighborhood, turning unproductive spaces into aspirational places where they could bring communities together. Then Stephen came across the concept of vertical walls, and suddenly they were growing plants in school and saving space.

They started growing edible plants in vertical planters at the school—the first indoor edible wall in a New York City school. That turned out to be brilliant, because then the kids could sell the foods in school. People could see it, and they could translate that success into other things. The green wall allowed the kids to experience success with other adults, not just Stephen.

For a long time, all of the other adults wanted Stephen to take those kids and get rid of them, take them somewhere else, move them, get them out of the school. Stephen wanted his kids to learn how to integrate with society and for teachers to learn to work with them as well, to set an example for others that anything is possible with these kids; it's how you deal with them and how you treat them. The green wall was the instrument that allowed them to build those relationships.

There's another component to all this. Stephen and his kids live in the heart of a food desert, where there is no access to fresh food whatsoever—an entire community with no supermarket. They shop in a bodega—twenty feet square and bulletproof, where all the food has unlimited shelf life.

So he took his kids out of the neighborhood to Whole Foods, and he says, "The craziest thing about going to Whole Foods with seventeen big teenage kids is that after security staff stopped following us around for the first half hour, we couldn't believe the amount of vegetables there were in the world. The kids were turning to me and saying, 'Mr. Ritz, I had no idea that there were so many different kinds of peppers and so many kinds of this.'"

Then they saw the customers paying $7, $8, $9 a pound for fresh produce, and the kids turned around and said, "You didn't teach us about this good stuff."

And from that day on, they never grew green peppers again. They started growing yellow peppers and red peppers and orange peppers, and Whole Foods was delighted to have them, and lo and behold, an economy was born. They never looked back.

Most importantly, all of those seventeen kids stayed out of jail. Not only did they stay out of jail, but they graduated high school and went on to post-secondary training and/or living-wage jobs.

Now with Tower Garden technology, the kids are growing enough food to generate 100 bags of groceries per week, fifty-two weeks a year, growing indoors with LED lights in the heart of a food desert. And the beauty of Tower Garden is that it's a replicable, scalable technology. Stephen is training teachers and embedding the work that they do into the curriculum so it becomes part of the daily school system.

Ten years ago, they couldn't name ten kinds of vegetables. Now they grow thirty-seven kinds of fruits and vegetables all year around, using 90 percent less water and 90 percent less space. "I love arugula and Asian eggplant," Stephen says, "but I didn't know. Who knew? It just goes to show you, a seed well planted and a crop well tended can give you a harvest of epic proportions."

Thirty thousand pounds of vegetables later, Stephen says his favorite crop is "organically grown citizens, graduates, members of the middle class; kids who are going to college and kids who aren't going to jail."

Make a Life

AT THE BEGINNING of each month in our organization, we assess where we are and where we're going with a series of three questions:

- *"What went well?" We celebrate the things we did well and make plans to continue doing them—strengthen them, in fact, so we can do them even better next month.*
- *"What went wrong?" We identify the obstacles we hit, the wrong paths we followed, and the things we should stop doing.*
- *Based on answers to the first two questions, we ask, "What should I do differently next month?"*

We answer the questions not to ourselves but to a coach or an accountability partner. If we build a rhythm of starting well and finishing strong, using an objective tool to assess ourselves with the help of an observer, we can make each month better than the month before as we make a life.

Then there is one more question: Was I receptive to any kairos moment that broke into my life? Did God drop an event or an opportunity or a relationship into my life that created an unexpected victory or crisis? What did I learn from that encounter? How can I be more sensitive to the next kairos moment?

I love the *Star Trek* opening that says, "Going boldly where no man has gone before." There are so many places we can go—places we would never think of on our own—if we let a new relationship with another person or our relationship with God build a bridge to take us there.

That's how we make a life.

About the Author

CURT BEAVERS has a passion for life. He and his wife, Lori, created a Juice Plus Virtual Franchise early in their marriage, which they continue to build. Through his work as a National Marketing Director for the Juice Plus Company, Curt has helped thousands of people around the world live healthier lives and build their own businesses.

Curt has cherished his role as a husband and father to their now-grown children, Trey, Hope, and Zach. While he was writing this book, Curt and Lori became grandparents for the first time. Reaching the next generation of his family, his business, and his church is Curt's passion—inspiring otheres to discover their own purpose, then pursue it with zeal. With his friend Tommy Newberry, he wrote *I Call Shotgun*, a series of letters on life to their sons.

A native of Atlanta, Georgia, Curt is a southern boy at heart, enjoying hunting and fishing, and also snow skiing, golf, and tennis. He loves the outdoors and the opportunity to acknowledge God as Creator.

Curt runs almost every day, a discipline that energizes him. He has a generous heart of hospitality, introducing friends to friends at every opportunity. This, he believes, is the greatest investment of relational capital.

And Curt pursues God in morning quiet time and throughout the day, attempting to live out Psalm 42:1: "As the deer pants for streams of water, so my soul pants for you, my God."

Curt would love to connect and help you on your journey to create the life you desire.

@curtbeavers

CurtBeavers.MakeALife

curt@makealife.com

makealife.com

CurtBeavers.com

"Some people like the 'Own your own business' p

trepreneur' part vs. owning your own business:

In today's culture, the concept of creating a *life* rather th

but ultimately unreachable. It is stored in a box that occa

if" and "that would be fun," only to pack it away again w

allows margin and fuel for the ignition of words like *hop*

had the courage to have dragged out of the box, dusted

about and prayed about. How blessed we have been to h

we are now living a *life* that allows us to chase our passior

— Ryan & Holly Morris • "Leading a life full of person

my dreams and schemes!" — Jeanette Votruba • Refu

WHAT DOES IT ME

through us can stir in this world. We catalyze *life* when w

the planet." — Scott Kindig • "It means having choice:

with. I feel blessed and fortunate that my 'work' is also m

work all about serving others and helping others achieve

themselves into discovering their gifts and abilities so th

Christofferson • "The assurance I have each morning t

that I am exactly where He wants me to be, serving othe

Caldwell • "To remain mindful, aware, and open to

Beavers • "Being able to pursue my passion of helping

physically, or financially by adding one piece of value to v